Praise for *Language for God*

"This book provides a thorough and accessible case for expansive and multifarious language and images for God. Weaving together personal narrative with a history of how we got here, alongside robust engagement in biblical and theological possibilities, Mary Streufert's *Language for God: A Lutheran Perspective* is to Lutheran theology in the twenty-first century what Elizabeth Johnson's *She Who Is* was to Catholic theology in the twentieth century. Grounded in the Lutheran tradition, this book is truly relevant for all people of faith, and for all those who have lost faith in the church's ability to include them."

—CARYN D. RISWOLD, professor of religion and the
Mike & Marge McCoy Family Distinguished Chair in
Lutheran Heritage and Mission, Wartburg College

"In this necessary book, Mary Streufert calls readers to reconsider and repent of the church's past and present use of almost exclusively male, white language and images for God. She powerfully calls for scriptural and theological faithfulness to the gospel through tapping into language and images for God that are feminine, masculine, and gender neutral. This book is a must-read for seminarians, lay leaders, pastors, and anyone who is a part of the life of the church."

—CRYSTAL L. HALL, Kraft Assistant Professor of Biblical Studies,
United Lutheran Seminary, and author of *Insights from
Reading the Bible with the Poor* (Fortress Press, 2019)

"With fascinating detail and an ear for significant stories, Streufert offers a careful argument and informing insights related to the significance and norms for imagery and language about God. Ironically, there are few book-length discussions of how Christians ought to speak to and about God, even though Christians and their communities have been debating this question for more than half a century. Streufert responds to this lacuna with a constructive theological proposal that calls for using multigendered terms and images. In six elegantly written chapters, she examines significant ways that the Bible and Christian tradition—including central themes in Luther's theology—offer support for moving beyond using only male terms and masculine imagery. I urge not only Christian pastors and theologians to study this book but also all persons who yearn to know, pray, and sing to God beyond the strictures of androcentrism."

—Kris Kvam, professor of theology, Saint Paul School of Theology, Kansas City and Oklahoma City, and author of *Eve and Adam: Jewish, Christian, and Muslim Readings of Genesis and Gender*

"In *Language for God*, Mary Streufert weaves wisdom from the work of Martin Luther, contemporary biblical studies, and historical anthropology. Most importantly, she maintains a clear focus on the question that should guide Christian theological reflection on language for God: How can our words and images for God best contribute to people hearing the good news of Jesus?"

—John Hoffmeyer, associate professor of systematic theology, United Lutheran Seminary, and author of *The Advent of Freedom: Time and Possibility in Hegel's Logic*

"In this fabulous book, Mary Streufert offers us 'new old ways to proclaim God for us.' Through careful investigation of the holy Scriptures, the ancient teachers of the church, the Christian and Lutheran tradition, and art she makes a convincing case for the need to, as she puts it: 'embrace language and images for God that are feminine, masculine, and neutral and at the same time scripturally, evangelically, and theologically faithful.' Preachers and teachers of the gospel will find in this book a wonderful resource for expanding the language available to proclaim the wonder of God's amazing love."

—Carmelo Santos, ELCA director for theological diversity and engagement and author of *Did God Create the Universe? A Bilingual Devotional for Kids with Big Questions*

Language for God

Language for God

A LUTHERAN PERSPECTIVE

Mary J. Streufert

Fortress Press
Minneapolis

LANGUAGE FOR GOD
A Lutheran Perspective

All Scripture quotations, unless otherwise indicated, are from New Revised Standard Version Bible, copyright © 1989 National Council of the Churches of Christ in the United States of America. Used by permission. All rights reserved worldwide.

Scripture quotations marked (KJV) are from the King James Version.

Cover image: 183362008 / iStockphoto.com
Cover design: Marti Naughton / sMartdesigN

Print ISBN: 978-1-5064-7396-3
eBook ISBN: 978-1-5064-7397-0

To
my teachers in faith:
my parents, Daniel and Donna Streufert;
Fred Niedner;
Theodore Ludwig;
Sarah DeMaris;
Marcus Borg;
Marjorie Hewitt Suchocki;
Jack Verheyden;
and
the friends and others whose stories I have held

Contents

Abbreviations

LW   *Luther's Works.* American Edition. Edited by Helmut T. Lehmann and Jaroslav Pelikan. 55 vols. St. Louis: Concordia; Philadelphia: Fortress, 1955–86.

TAL *The Annotated Luther.* Edited by Hans J. Hillerbrand, Kirsi I. Stjerna, and Timothy J. Wengert. 6 vols. Minneapolis: Fortress, 2015–17.

WA   *D. Martin Luthers Werke: Kritische Gesamtausgabe.* Edited by J. K. F. Knaake. 109 vols. Weimar: H. Böhlau, 1883–2009.

Introduction

To whom will you liken me and make me equal,
and compare me, as though we were alike?

—Isaiah 46:5

When I was four years old, I wanted to be a pastor. I put my witch dress from the previous Halloween to good use. My mom had sewn me a long black witch's dress with fringe and swooping sleeves, and she crafted a pointy hat trimmed with the same fringe. That dress was my cassock. I assembled my dolls and animals at the head of my little brown youth bed, and I upended my pale-green doll bed for my pulpit. I put my mom's confirmation King James Bible on the upended headboard. And I preached. I had no inkling my church didn't allow me to preach because of my body.

When I think back to that time when my family was part of a small congregation in Oklahoma, I recall no clear understanding of God through language or visual images. I only remember sensibilities about God—calm, peace, beauty, stillness. Those moments weren't from someone telling me about God. Instead, I remember my sensibilities about God through the way I felt sitting in the dark pews in church, with a drama going on up front. Or in the soaring ceiling of the darkened fellowship hall that echoed when I was alone in it. Or in the stillness I felt in my pink bedroom, where light made the room different throughout the day. Why do I have no overwhelming memory as a small child of God as Father, Jesus as Son, and both as He—capital *H*?

My only guess is that the things that shaped me gave me something different in faith.

Maybe there was no way I wouldn't have wanted to be a pastor. My dad was a pastor; my mom was a writer, schoolteacher, and women's leader. My paternal grandpa taught German in Missouri Synod schools in St. Louis for decades; my grandma eventually worked in the denomination's office there. My uncles and great-uncles were pastors. And yet, at four, I had not learned my secondary role in the church or in the world.

Maybe images told me something. In an archival dig in my basement a few years ago, I found all my preschool Sunday school handouts. Colorful oil drawings take the whole eight-and-a-half-by-eleven-inch cover page. Two things work against each other in the artwork. All the biblical characters are white—maybe some are Middle Eastern. Maybe. Black families and children are in the contemporary pictures *inside* the handout but never on the cover.

At the same time, white or Middle Eastern women and girls are the central figures—or only figures—on many of the covers. Even the unnamed slave girl in Naaman's household is a cover figure, along with Naaman's wife (2 Kgs 5). What the girl did—her faith—is the point of the story about Naaman. What God did through her matters.

Of course, Sunday school wasn't the only influence. I looked at books all the time at home, including Arch Books. Until last year when I ran out of space, I kept them on my shelves. Before packing them up for safekeeping, I did a quick gender analysis of them. In roughly equal thirds, they came out like this: centrally male-identified characters, both male- and female-identified characters, and centrally female-identified characters. These are the images I looked at on my own in my pink bedroom where the light changed the room all day long. Images are, of course, what seeing people see with their eyes. Images are also what we produce in our imaginations. We produce images through stories, through music, through what we do, and through how we worship. We evoke images with our words.

There was church too. Back then, the pastor did everything but collect the offering. He read the Scriptures, preached the sermon, prayed the prayers of the people, and distributed communion. And as I said, he was my dad. I recall no cognitive dissonance between what he did in the holy space at St. John Lutheran and what I rehearsed in my pink bedroom. I was too young to read when we lived in Oklahoma, so I learned the liturgy first by immersion—something like foreign-language immersion because I was *in* the liturgy and could eventually sing it without thinking about it, without knowing, at least fully, what it all meant. What images did the words of the liturgy evoke?

The biblical imagery of God as King and Father and Jesus as Lamb and Son resound in the sung liturgy, and while I know that the liturgy of my childhood is an ancient liturgy, not a specifically Lutheran liturgy, the masculine identity of God, Jesus Christ, and Christians is in retrospect overwhelming. What is beautiful is this: the liturgy that became one of my languages also sings, confesses, and otherwise proclaims intimate dependence on God and God's Triune identity. I carry a deep knowledge of all creaturely dependence on the Creator of the universe, particularly my own dependence. I'm not in charge, and I stand before God and neighbor alike. But in the foreign language of the liturgy that I absorbed, God was a white man, and Jesus was a white man.

For good and for ill, these are some of what Black liberation theologian James Cone calls the "nonintellectual factors" that shaped me. In 1975, not long after my bedroom preaching, Cone revealed some of his own nonintellectual factors to demonstrate how they are often the source of theologians' perspectives and methods.[1] You have them too—factors that are nonintellectual and intellectual alike. Some are positive, some neutral or negative. Some are historical events, rupturing, comforting, or otherwise. Some are the games we play, the people we know, or the music we make. Some are deeply personal, others highly public. Some are stories or artwork. Some factors have to do with language, written, said, signed, sung, dramatized, and implied. And some factors that shape us are the language and images we have for God.

In this book, I explore Christian language and images for God because they have been overwhelmingly masculine and white. I would call this a factor that affects everyone, no matter your beliefs. In 2006, I was called into the responsibility to assist the Evangelical Lutheran Church in America (ELCA) to address sexism in church and society. Those exact words were in my job description. Through many years of work to assist this church in its responsibility, I have seen a connection between faith and life, theology and action. As the National Council of Churches (NCC) Justice for Women Working Group communicated in its 2011 Words Matter initiative, words for God matter.[2]

Through the 2019 ELCA Churchwide Assembly, this church affirmed social teaching that declares patriarchy and sexism as sinful and calls on ELCA bishops, synods, and the churchwide organization to use gender-inclusive language for God.[3] We need to reflect theologically together. Think about what you know through language for God. I wonder if God had been understood with words and images that related to my little four-year-old female-identified body, maybe I would not have been considered illegitimate for ministry.

But what does the Bible say? Let's start with a few images for the backs of our minds. In Luke 15, the Pharisees and the scribes were "grumbling" about Jesus because he welcomed "sinners" and ate with them. Who your table partners were defined your status in the ancient world. It was a big deal. People who were "high" in the social strata would not eat with those who were "low." Jesus's dining practices did away with the parameters people expected, and this drove some of the religious leaders crazy. They called Jesus's table partners "sinners." They were mad. Jesus was hosting parties of social disrupters, people he invited to go against the controls of the social hierarchy by eating together.[4] So what does Jesus do to defuse the grumblers' grumbling? He tells two stories. The Christian tradition has remembered and revered the first one and forgotten or largely ignored the second one.

The first one is of a shepherd and a sheep:

> So he told them this parable: "Which one of you, having a hundred sheep and losing one of them, does not leave the ninety-nine in the wilderness and go after the one that is lost until he finds it? When he has found it, he lays it on his shoulders and rejoices. And when he comes home, he calls together his friends and neighbors, saying to them, 'Rejoice with me, for I have found my sheep that was lost.' Just so, I tell you, there will be more joy in heaven over one sinner who repents than over ninety-nine righteous persons who need no repentance." (Luke 15:3–7)

Most of us stop there. Jesus is the Good Shepherd; we are the lost sheep. We pray with these words. We sing with these words. We talk this way about faith. A lot.

But there is no break in the text. The second one is of a householder and a coin:

> Or what woman having ten silver coins, if she loses one of them, does not light a lamp, sweep the house, and search carefully until she finds it? When she has found it, she calls together her friends

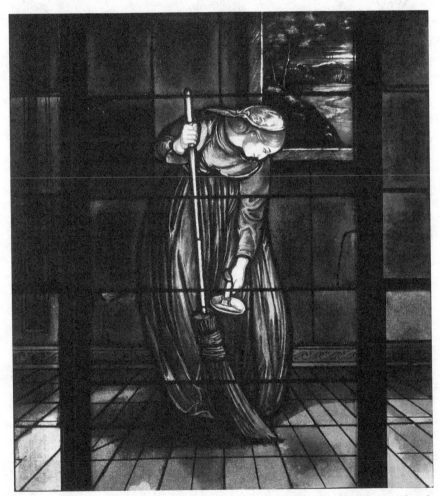

Figure I.1. "The Good Householder" stained glass window, St. Jacob Lutheran Church in Anna, Ohio. Ludwig Von Gerichten, artist. Photograph by Mary Ann Klopfleisch. Used by permission.

and neighbors, saying, "Rejoice with me, for I have found the coin that I had lost." Just so, I tell you, there is joy in the presence of the angels of God over one sinner who repents. (Luke 15:8–10)

We must have the rest of the story. Jesus is the Good Householder; we are the lost coin. We don't pray with these words. We don't sing with these words. We don't talk this way about faith. Hardly ever.

Why?

During an adult education forum with a congregation in St. Louis, some folks gasped and leaned into their video cameras when I said, "Imagine what difference it would make if the woman and the coin were in our chancels—just as often as the shepherd is." They were hungry to imagine. Some people have already. St. Jacob Lutheran Church in Anna, Ohio, has a stained-glass window of her. What if all Christians did, not only in our chancels, but in our hearts and minds? And in our liturgies?

This is what I invite you into. I want to open things I have found in the past. I think we can see the present through some of it. Thinking about history in conversation with Lutheran theology also helps us make sense of Christian language and images for God that are of every gender. From a Lutheran perspective, language for God matters.

1 The Church and Language for God

The church is a storehouse of memories and stories, big and small. . . .
We cannot be anything but translators and storytellers. That is how we
can be the church.

—Mary (Joy) Philip, "The Elusive Lure of the Lotus,"
in *Transformative Lutheran Theologies*

Language and images for God, I am convinced, matter for our deepest longings in faith. You might pause and reflect, When I think about faith, what
do I long for? What are my deepest yearnings in my relationship with God?
What do I notice when I rest in quiet for a moment?

I've heard some of these yearnings of faith. As humans, we live in the
tender folds of strength and weakness. Often it seems we do not share
the memories and stories of our needs. But we have needy hearts and clamor-
ing minds; our spirits search for the comfort of being truly known and loved.
As the psalmist writes, "O God, you are my God, I seek you, my soul thirsts
for you; my flesh faints for you, as in a dry and weary land where there is no
water" (Ps 63:1). We live unsettled and searching. Here are a few of the stories
and memories of the church I have heard. Maybe your story of yearning in
faith fits here too.

The room was dim so that we could see the slides on the screen. It was
one of the first times I shared images of Jesus Christ that were unfamiliar
to many North American Christians—Jesus as Asian, Middle Eastern, or
American Indian. These were paintings by artists in the twentieth century.
In other images, Jesus Christ did not look clearly masculine, and in still

others, Jesus appeared to be pregnant or depicted with symbols of nursing. Those were by artists in the eleventh to the sixteenth century.

The lights came on, and people were curious, talkative. I wrapped up the session. From the back of the room, Magdalena shot to the front. We had talked the previous day. But this time she had tears in her eyes. Her body was taut, engaged. "I saw Jesus like me. I didn't know these images existed!" Like her, meaning seemingly masculine and feminine. Seeing Jesus with a beard but pregnant was new, even though the images are hundreds of years old. "I didn't know I needed to see this."

Another time, no one spoke to me, but I saw body language. I was in Oklahoma for a synod assembly, and in a keynote address on a topic not related to language and images for God, I used an image of Jesus Christ as American Indian. When it went on the screen, I could see it affect an older man and a young man in the back row. Their seeing Jesus like them changed me. I am guessing that they had seen images like this before. I am guessing God is not white for them. Yet in a white-identified space, Jesus Christ was shown as American Indian. Their recognition told me again how we yearn in faith.

It kept happening, this yearning unearthed. With tears in his eyes, a Lutheran bishop told me on the last day of a conference that he and his spouse had been skeptical about what images and language for Jesus I would share. Jesus like a woman? And these paintings are how old? In the middle of it, they found themselves fed, surprised, grateful. The symbols of Jesus Christ as the source of the church are sometimes portrayed as Jesus pregnant. One image in an illustrated Bible in the medieval era even shows a church building being birthed from Jesus's side. These were powerful teaching images in a time when few people could read.

At the same conference, an older couple drifted to my side while we waited for the doors to open for worship. I got a little nervous. It was 2014, and it was not popular to be a feminist Lutheran in church circles. One of them passed me a handwritten note and said how grateful they were to see images of Jesus Christ that disrupted our ideas about gender because they have a transgender child. It seemed they experienced being opened up, affirmed. They felt that their child was loved in a new way. I still have the note.

A year later, a young pastor approached me after a session. His face was flushed. I watched him blink at his tears. "Thank you. I didn't know what to do with how I felt left out when my wife nursed our baby. But these symbols of Jesus help me, and I feel closer to my child and wife now." He stopped for a moment but then continued, "I had no idea these were out there! Where can I find them?"

People yearn in faith to be known and loved and fed. Each person I met was surprised by their own responses. As humans, I think we respond to being known. As Christians, I think we respond to the God who is *for us* in all our human complexities and all our difference and alikeness. Images of Jesus portrayed in many ethnicities and being a mix of genders reached people who did not even expect to have their yearnings in faith met this way. They were caught off guard by God made known to them in unexpected ways. And they were grateful. But I have also heard yearnings that didn't surprise people. Others were distinctly aware of their yearnings in faith. These are just a few of those stories.

"I decided I'm not going to cry tears of anguish and shame in church anymore," my friend Tara told me. The nearly total masculine and male-identified language and images for God, she said, were completely interfering with her faith. Worship met none of her faith yearnings. She heard no gospel declared in her language. For years the masculine language in the liturgy made it not worship for her. Anger and sorrow gripped her body, and she would struggle to make sure her tears were discreet. Things changed once she cried openly during a service and was no longer trying to be polite by hiding her pain. The open sorrow of her heart finally allowed her to move away from Lutheran worship to a different Christian church. Full of despair, she sought inclusive language for God and finally made the painful decision with her spouse to transfer their family membership from their church home of over twenty years. That exodus, she told me, remains the most agonizing loss of her adult life. But she shouldn't have had to leave to be fed.

My friend Jean struggled too. She didn't just leave the Lutheran tradition; she left Christianity, in part because of language for God. Because others did not yearn for language for God that was not nearly exclusively masculine, she felt alone in the community of faith. No one, it seemed, felt the same yearning to hear God proclaimed as feminine as well as masculine. Was there no one to search with her?

A woman in an online conference last year told me how tired she was of waiting for the church to use feminine language for God. Her simple admission crackled through the internet. She didn't have to say much for me to feel the ribbons of yearning spooled deep within her. She is still waiting to hear the gospel in language that fully speaks to her.

None of this loss in faith is necessary.

The Problem

The problem is that God is a man in much Christian imagination. Christians use mostly masculine-identified language and stories and images. One word to describe this predominant Christian conception of God is *androcentric*: it is male identified and male centered.

I am interested in understanding why. History provides clues. As Lutheran church historian Susan McArver says, "History is to an institution what memory is to an individual."[1] History helps us make sense of why we do things and who we are. History reveals a powerful link between how people define bodies and behaviors associated with sex and gender and language and images for God. But what do I mean by *sex*? Although sexuality is intertwined with sex and gender, *sex* here refers to bodies, not our physical relationships. For example, in the United States right now, reproductive organs usually define a person's sex. *Gender* refers to how we express or identify ourselves or cultural expectations based on sex. Simply put, the history of sex and gender that we have inherited in the United States and in the Lutheran tradition is that men are superior. It is a history likewise intertwined with white supremacy.

If you look at it closely enough, the history of the United States reveals a trail of evidence that female bodies and Black and brown bodies matter far less than male bodies and white bodies.[2] When people are perceived and treated as inferior to others, they suffer and often die. For hundreds of years, prophets and scholars have been working to unravel this problem.[3] Historical study shows that while distinct, they are intertwined. To talk about language for God that is of all genders, I will explore some of this intersected history, even while I focus on the problems related to *gendered* language for God.

In this century, some famous people are using their power to point out how religion contributes to problems for women and girls and to cultivate change. Former president Jimmy Carter wrote a book about the connection between religion and violence against women and girls after he gathered global faith leaders to take this connection seriously. Carter wants religious leaders to be part of the effort to care for everyone's well-being. Grounded in his Baptist faith, Carter urges everyone to take account of the ways religion supports sexism—and then to do something about it.[4]

In her efforts to stem gender-based poverty, Melinda Gates calls on religious leaders to amplify female-identified voices in faith traditions because from her point of view, the poverty many women experience is deeply connected to the role religion plays in their lives. What religions say about women and girls—that they are inferior to men and boys—seeps into everyone's consciousness, she argues, whether someone is a girl, a boy, or a queer person. And, she continues, while it is not her job to trace the sources of the problems women and girls experience due to religion, religious people and churches need to trace these issues and respond to them.[5] Many people of faith have been trying to do just this for decades.

Protestant church bodies have been shifting language for God in worship, some more recently than others. For instance, beginning in 1973, the United Church of Christ (UCC) was among the first church bodies to discuss and call for decreasing the frequency of masculine language for God.[6] The UCC made inclusive-language resources available beginning in 1981.[7] In 2018, the General Convention of the Episcopal Church voted to provide gender-neutral options for language for God in three prayers in one order of liturgy.[8]

Even before the ELCA was formed by joining together separate Lutheran church bodies in the United States, Lutheran churches were trying to shift Lutheran practices.[9] Scholars, educators, and others collaborated to encourage Lutherans to know and experience both human and divine identity untethered from androcentrism.

In the 1970s, predecessor bodies of the ELCA acted to create changes in language. Some of the institutional recommendations included advice that continues to be relevant. For example, the Church Council of the American Lutheran Church (ALC) resolved in 1976, "More inclusive symbols and language referring to God are also encouraged so that materials reflect the male/female wholeness of the Christian community and the all-encompassing nature of God."[10] In the 1980s, significant Lutheran scholarship on language for God emerged. For example, Gail Ramshaw offered a clarion call in 1982: "It is time to break the model of God-he. . . . If increasingly in American English 'he' denotes male sexuality [sex], it becomes a simple matter of idolatry to refer to God as 'he.'"[11] Men also felt urgencies to challenge androcentric language for God. Five years later, H. Frederick Reisz Jr. wrote, "I urge the pastoral *expansion* of the language we use for God, retaining in some places and times 'Father and Son,' and using other words at other times. . . . Images address God and then are broken by God's Word. I am humble enough to know that all these words and images are not God, and I do see through a veil darkly."[12]

Likewise, scholarship on language influenced the early years of the ELCA. In 1989, the Office of the Secretary and the Commission for Communication created and released the document *Guidelines for Inclusive Use of the English Language for Speakers, Writers and Editors*. It contains advice not only for humankind but also for God. Human speech about God, the guide stresses, must express God's mercy. Although the guide acknowledges Jesus's address to God as Father, the authors clearly encourage people to avoid nearly exclusive masculine language for God because of its effect on faith.[13] Instead, the guide advocates for a multiplicity of images. The guide was withdrawn from widespread use after some people protested it. The ELCA's history related to language for God reveals opposing viewpoints on whether God is masculine or not.

What happened in the ELCA reflects what was happening across Christianity. In the 1990s, discussion about language for God became highly charged. Women collaborated in ecumenical circles to push for female-identified liturgical language and practices. Scholars published books both for and against female-identified language. In some ways, the conversation became shouting matches, with some claiming heresy on one side and patriarchy on the other. But scholars were not the only ones in the debates; congregations, pastors, and bishops entered the fray as well. For some people and communities today, the debate is not over. And therefore, the need continues, and the discussion is not over either.

Lutherans have been working for decades to take account of the interface between religion and sexism not only in the United States but worldwide. The Lutheran World Federation (LWF) has a gender justice policy.[14] It emphasizes inclusion and equity as Christian values rooted in Lutheran expressions of faith, and it gives practical suggestions for communities of faith and agencies. Lutherans all over the world use this document, and many leaders and activists collaborate regularly to generate action and coordinate efforts and ideas. Many of these leaders and activists underscore how important it is to live in faith with language and ideas that do not hurt people.

Another important step is the ELCA's social statement *Faith, Sexism, and Justice: A Call to Action.* Social statements from this church rely on the Scriptures and theology to develop a Lutheran ethical vision about an issue. The social statement task force's responsibility was to study, discuss, and write about the ways sexism hurts women and girls, but what they discovered was that sexism hurts everyone. Through their seven years of collaboration, they came to recognize an extensive history of sexism that continues to influence everything from paychecks to parenting to pulpits.

Through its churchwide assembly in 2019, the ELCA adopted this teaching and policy statement, which declares patriarchy and sexism sinful because they foil God's desire for abundance and justice. The statement also explains that language for God that is mostly male oriented can hurt faith and hurt people. It hurts faith by narrowing "an understanding of God to the figure of an infinitely powerful man." It hurts people by giving the message "that men have more in common with God."[15]

What I have found is that in a worldview where men are considered superior, God is not "allowed" to be feminine or female identified. As feminist scholar Mary Daly famously said, "If God is male, then male is God."[16] The reasoning is that if God is the best, God cannot be identified with anything female or feminine because they are supposedly not the best. Similarly, in a worldview where white people are superior, God is not "allowed" to be Black or brown. As my colleague Kathryn riffed on Daly, "If God is white, then white is God." When female and Black and brown bodies are perceived and treated as inferior to male and white bodies, God is portrayed and prayed to as if God were a white man. In other words, androcentric language for God is theologically and pastorally harmful. But the Scriptures and the Lutheran tradition tell us something more complex and more beautiful than this.

As the stories I have shared illustrate, understanding God nearly exclusively as a white man interferes with faith for many people. In other words, androcentric language for God is a deficiency for Christian evangelism. Always referring to God the Father and God the Son and using masculine pronouns or even avoiding them altogether gets in the way of effective proclamation of the gospel. It's not evangelical. Language and images for God matter not only for our deepest longings in faith as individuals but also for publicly professed faith. How we imagine God and speak to God in worship matters. These words and images for God matter for all forms of human flourishing.

A Way Forward

From my perspective, the answer to the problem of androcentric language for the three persons of the Trinity comes from faith itself. As I have said, people need the gospel in language that proclaims to them. The proclamation that God is *for us* will include language and images for God that come from many genders and no gender at all. It is scripturally, evangelically, and theologically faithful to use language for God that is simultaneously masculine, feminine, and neutral. Some people might call the use of multiple gender references for God as language that "queers" the sex binary in language. That is, this kind of language disrupts or queers the idea of opposite sexes or opposite genders. Here I will refer to language that is masculine, feminine, and neutral as *multigendered*.

My proposal for what I am calling multigendered language and images for God is not about canceling masculine language. It is about unhinging Christian language for God from almost entirely masculine language or gender-neutral language in favor of multiple genders, not only in personal devotion, but in public faith, from worship to Bible study to Christian education. Multigendered language for God is not only scriptural but also central to effective evangelism and faithful to several central convictions Martin Luther stressed.

Where can we find this language? I think we have it already—in Scripture and in the Christian theological tradition. We just need to be confident to use it. We need to put God's love into language people need and are themselves using. Luther, for one, did not tell the German people to learn a different language in order to receive the gospel. He argued that liturgy and sermons needed to be in language people knew. And he translated the Bible into German. He claimed that all people, not just a few trained clerics, had the responsibility of making the gospel known—that is, telling the gospel story. People who proclaim the gospel, Luther thought, needed to listen closely to how people they minister to talk, even when their talking is without words. Translations and texts need to be fashioned for people who will find themselves surprised but nevertheless fed by multigendered language and images for God. And sometimes the "translation" needs to be for people who already know their hunger, their yearnings in faith. Yet the translation is always about God's love for us.

Arguments for Inclusive Language for God

What have scholars said about language for God? Scholars have been researching and writing about language for God for a long time. For example, some scholars argue that Christianity itself is too patriarchal, too identified with and dominated by men, to serve anyone but men well. They think women and others should leave the church to be fed elsewhere.[17] Others argue that Christianity needs to be transformed from within. They urge Christians to embrace and practice language for God and for people that includes all genders and races and to support teachings that do not crush women and people from racialized and minoritized communities.[18]

Scholars write about language for God within many different countries. Three of the many well-known writers on the subject are Brian Wren, who comes out of the United Reformed Church (UK); Elizabeth A. Johnson, a Roman Catholic; and Gail Ramshaw, who is Lutheran. Writing in 1989, Wren argued that the ways we understand and live out masculinity, including the idea of male dominance, is a faith issue for everyone. He studied language as a poet and linguist and came to the conclusion that language for God is so central to faith for Christians that we need to, as he wrote, "bring many names" for God to worship.[19] He writes hymns to fulfill this commitment.

Elizabeth Johnson explored the problem of women's oppression, both historically and within religion. She listened to women weeping. She saw their oppression, which is, she argued, reinforced by androcentric language for God. She then took her insights into influential Roman Catholic figures such as Saints Augustine and Thomas Aquinas to argue that the Holy Trinity is also female identified.[20] She does not leave her faith tradition but instead pushes it to be read and understood anew. Learning from feminist, womanist, and *mujerista* theologians from many Christian traditions, she seeks to strengthen her own faith tradition.

Gail Ramshaw has been writing since the 1970s for both Lutheran and ecumenical audiences. She continues to encourage and inspire language for God that comes from as many biblical images as possible. Ramshaw has written dozens of books and articles on language for God and worship, starting in the 1980s. Her work opens Christians to the scriptural and theological reasons for inclusive and expansive language for God, and she offers rich guidance for worship, communal study, and personal devotion.

Arguments against Inclusive Language for God

Being familiar with the basic arguments of critics clarifies why I say what I do in this book. Broadly speaking, critics of inclusive language and images for God respond to it by saying that feminism erodes faith and that with feminism, the gospel will be lost. They fear the loss of faith in God's promise.

It seems to me that what critics of inclusive language are saying boils down to two basic themes: the Bible and revelation. Regarding the Bible, they think that feminists (and others) use Scripture selectively, that they rework Scripture to align with their perspectives. Critics further conclude that using gender-inclusive language and images for God ignores the literal meaning of the text and thus undermines the authority of Scripture.

The other basic theme is revelation. Critics argue that the Scriptures reveal the three persons of the Trinity as masculine and male identified. They argue that the Bible reveals Jesus to be the incarnate Son of God. And Jesus refers to God as Father and the Holy Spirit as masculine. To suggest otherwise or to replace this language with something else muddies revelation, they think.

The bottom line from this collective viewpoint is that the Triune God is masculine. One evangelical scholar argues that Jesus Christ as savior is "properly portrayed as masculine" and that Jesus revealed as God "himself" as a man is not a biological argument.[21] He argues that God acts like a man should in a world with two opposite sexes and that God as the masculine "side" of this two-sex world is all about God's being, not about biology. At the same time, pointing to the writings of Julian of Norwich, this same critic claims Christ as nurturer can be feminine. Taken all together, his argument implies that whatever is masculine or male can be both "properly" masculine and also generic, somehow without sex and gender implications.[22]

Critics connect several other intertwined arguments to their assertion that God is revealed as masculine. These arguments are about sexuality and God's being, the faith of Jesus, God's name, and God's embodied life in the incarnation.

Some Lutheran and evangelical theologians argue against female-identified and feminine language and images for God because, they claim, sexuality cannot be "introduced" or "confused" into the Godhead. Some of them say that addressing God as Mother will make God a goddess.[23] They say that Father and Son include the feminine. One critic states, "Fatherhood in the biblical context includes motherhood, and Sonship encompasses certain nuances of meaning associated with daughters."[24]

Critics link arguments about sexuality with arguments about God's being, which in philosophy and theology are called ontological arguments. Saying that we cannot ascribe sexuality to God and that God as Mother makes God sexual, they argue that God as Father is "nearly literal," meaning that God as Father and Son is not from human experience but is literally about God's very being—and somehow unhinged from sex, gender, and sexuality. In essence, they argue that "Father" and "Son" are objective references, having nothing to do with human value judgments or human realities.

One Lutheran scholar even makes a very non-Lutheran argument by saying that women are superior in their being because, he says, sexuality and sexual reproduction are linked together for women in a way that they are not for men. He argues that because women are superior beings, God should be understood as masculine.[25]

Another argument related to concerns about revelation is the claim that gender-inclusive language for God is not messianic, that it is not faithful to "the messianic faith of Jesus in His God and heavenly Father."[26] Critics are worried that calling upon God as Mother and referring to God as She makes God abstract and remote and is not the active and self-revealed God of the Scriptures. This is a concern that ties directly to arguments about the name of God.

Basically, critics state that anything but masculine language for God and God known as Father, Son, and Holy Spirit is heretical. This is, of course, a strong charge. But it stems from a deeply felt concern. They do not want a God that is different from the God of Scriptures, since the biblical languages themselves use these masculine nouns and pronouns.

One Lutheran critic states that feminist criticism of androcentric language and images for God puts God dangerously beyond embodied life, beyond the incarnation,[27] and thus beyond the doctrine of the Trinity. He is worried that the way Christians understand God's life in the three persons of the Trinity (what is called the immanent Trinity—the relationship within the threefold relations of the Trinity) will be lost, that Christians will no longer understand God as relational. He also is worried that the way Christians understand the threefold activity of the Trinity to create, redeem, and sanctify (what is called the economic Trinity—the way God is "capable" of history) will be lost, that Christians will no longer understand that the three persons of the Trinity don't have separate jobs, so to speak.[28] The doctrine of the Trinity explains that the first person, second person, and third person of the Trinity each and all create, redeem, and sanctify—not that the first person creates, the second person redeems, and the third person sanctifies.

Where Do We Go from Here?

Not surprisingly, my views are contrary to these critiques. By listening to people's needs, by studying the Scriptures, history, and the Lutheran theological tradition, I see *people* being lost, not the gospel. People's needs in faith are not being met because of the overwhelming masculine identity of the Christian tradition and language and images for God.

Rejecting the Bible might be on the minds of some feminist Christians, but in my experience, it is on the minds of very few. Most, and I include myself here, are reading, talking, and searching in an ongoing endeavor to live in faith, to support faithfulness to the Triune God who is for us, and to challenge what makes faith crumble for people. For me, Scripture matters.

Christianity has a long tradition of living faith "from the margins." Faith from the margins includes reading the Bible from the margins. Starting in the 1960s, laypeople, theologians, and biblical scholars in grassroots Bible study circles in Central and South America began to read the Bible "from the margins." They were eventually called liberation theologians. Christian liberation theology is now considered a regularized category, but its adherents do not necessarily have the same life experiences and perspectives, and they are not always the loudest voices or the most influential in the Christian tradition. Liberation theology also includes Spanish-speaking women in the United States writing as *mujerista* theologians, Korean theologians, queer theologians, and womanist theologians. And liberation theology includes feminist theologians reading from the margins.

One commonality among these liberation voices is a focus on wrestling with the tradition to make sense of faith from within their lives. In other words, people who read the Bible from the margins seek understanding from within the lived experience of faith. Faith is seen not so much as adherence to doctrines as it is a contextual response to God's Word. Reading from the margins prioritizes God's concern for all who are marginalized, including those who feel marginalized by language for God that is not fully inclusive.

My aim in this book is to add to the conversation and the growth and curiosity we have as people of faith who seek understanding. James Cone did this. His experiences as a Black boy living under the shadow of white supremacy in Arkansas shaped his theology. In one of his last publications, which is more autobiographical than his others, he writes about his drive to seek theological meaning that would help others. He asks, "How could I find meaning in a world that ignored black people?"[29] He wrote for himself and has become a voice for many others.

In a similar way, I am driven to ask how women, girls, and female-identified, femme, and queer folks find meaning in language and images for the three persons of the Trinity, especially if the language excludes them, making them invisible. And I ask this question as a specific person shaped by intersections of systems of oppression in ways similar to and different from some of you. Some of these shaping factors are obvious, and some are hidden, yet all the aspects of who I am are some of the "nonintellectual factors," as James Cone refers to them, that influence my theology. This is why, for example, I talk about my own life, but I do so to help you think about your life too. In addition to thinking individually, however, Christians need to think together, as communities in dialogue with the past, present, and future of the Christian tradition.

I offer a specifically Lutheran perspective on language for God because I think that some of Luther's insights are central to multigendered language and images for God. Simply put, I think Lutherans need some Lutheran reasons to proclaim the grace of God in feminine language. I hope, however, that this Lutheran perspective serves all Christians who need further scriptural and theological insights into the faithfulness of language for God that is multigendered. Much of Luther's biblical and theological insight continues to shape Christian faith and the church worldwide. My conclusions will seem outrageous to some and sensible to others, heretical to some and faithful to others.

Historically, language for God has tended to be primarily masculine. In chapters 2 and 3, I explore one stream in the history of sex (not sexuality) and gender to show how human understandings of people permeate Christian symbols and faith. Saying that feminine or female-identified language and images for God is a problem because it introduces sexuality into the Godhead relies on historical definitions of females as highly sexualized temptations and males as somehow "neutral" humans. Both ancient and more recent ways to understand sex and gender support males as "up" in rank and as "legitimate" humans and females as "down" in rank and as "illegitimate" humans. The Christian tradition has largely treated gendered symbols for God the same way. Christian faith does not need to be beholden to this history.

The Lutheran tradition serves as a compass, a tool for orientation on a way forward. In chapters 4 and 5, I take a close look at Martin Luther's life and theology. Understood in context, Luther as pastor, scholar, father, and spouse embodied challenges to devaluing women and girls. Some aspects of his life even serve as a guide in reforming androcentric language for humans and for God. But his theology is the true compass. Although his theology sometimes repeats and reinforces male authority and the androcentrism of the Christian tradition, at the same time, some of his own key teachings serve to fracture it. What Luther had to say about religious language, the proclamation of the gospel, the Word of God, and justification by grace through faith serves to reform language for God to be inclusive—that is, to be multigendered.

In chapter 6, I turn to Lutheran biblical interpretation and how it helps us read the Scriptures. We find images for God and people that disrupt gender stereotypes and any expectations that sex and gender are only a binary of opposites, for God or human creatures. As I will show, the Scriptures hold not only feminine and female-identified language and images but also powerful messages about gender disruption in views of God and of humans.

In the conclusion, I come back around to some of the central themes I think help Christians faithfully affirm God as both hidden and revealed, who may be spoken to and of in multigendered language and images.

As you move into these chapters, it might be helpful to have an image of my method in mind, which makes sense through the metaphor of music. How I listen to music has changed over the years, and this experience helps me explain part of what I do as a feminist Lutheran theologian. Since I was eleven years old, I have played the clarinet. From grade school through university, I almost always played the first part in concert bands, marching bands, and orchestras. This means that I regularly played the melody. I certainly heard other parts around me and was aware of the total sound we created as a band or an orchestra. But until my own children played music, I did not fully appreciate what it means to pay close attention to the harmonic parts or to other counterparts. I did not fully know what it was like to listen for a particular instrument that does not usually play the melody all the way through a piece of music.

Once my oldest child started to play the baritone saxophone, my ears always sought his line of music in every piece. I realized that my listening was different and that my experience of the total piece was different because

I started to hear a particular voice within the whole, one that had always been there but one I had not paid attention to. Because I heard the baritone sax more clearly, I heard the whole piece of music differently. Then my second child started to play percussion. Listening specifically, even lovingly, to percussion completely changed how I experienced and understood whole pieces of music once again. After learning to listen for certain parts, I wasn't so focused on the melody any longer. But then my third child started to play the trumpet, which often carries the melody, teaching me to hear all three parts in their divergence as a complex whole.

For me, this is what feminist theology is like. It often involves listening closely to a voice, element, or subject that is not the prevailing one in order to know the whole in a new way. In music or theology, listening in this way can make the experience more complex and more divergent but also more unified because of being attuned to greater complexity. Discovering something new becomes a possibility. It is in this very way I approach the Lutheran theological tradition and Scripture as a feminist Lutheran theologian. I pay attention to elements that are perhaps less obvious in both. This is how, I suggest, we will arrive at understanding inclusive language for God as scripturally, evangelically, and theologically faithful, even necessary. I read between the lines, which, as one biblical scholar I write about in chapter 6 explains, is a method for interpreting the Gospel of Luke. I listen for themes that are not always easily detected, especially if you are mostly accustomed to hearing the predominant themes.

You might be wondering why I'm focusing so much on Luther then. Why not rely mostly on people from more recent times and any place but Europe? This is a fair question. The many voices of the Lutheran theological tradition matter. I think part of the beauty of the ongoing Lutheran tradition is our diversity and the ways we try to simply "sit" with our differences, something I wrote about and hold dear in the streams of queer, womanist, *mujerista*, and feminist Lutheran theologies.[30] But why Luther when I am talking about sex and gender and race?

Because of his pivotal role in the emergence of the Protestant church, Luther remains a conversation partner. As with other theologians dead and alive, we're simply talking. And listening. We're engaged in a rather lengthy conversation about faith and what really matters. Christians, each a theologian of one sort or another, keep talking with one another, and with this talking, we act and continue to be part of the church that is always being reformed—by God. My essential point is that Luther's life and writing are thick resources for insight. And as the self-proclaimed reluctant founder of the Lutheran tradition, he remains our partner in mutual conversation. Luther has reforming insights that continue to matter.

I am part of the Lutheran tradition and claim it as a gift. And I think this tradition is a guide to answer how to make visible language for God in multiple genders. I urge ongoing reformation in this tradition to serve the free course of the gospel, to give witness to the God on whom we as Christians say we completely depend.

My friend Paul and I were in conversation. He was once my family's pastor and asked what I wanted this book to do. I really like arguments—not the kind that use antagonism and fury but the kind that rely on sources and logic and experience. My friend, I was pretty certain, does not spend lots of time thinking about language for God. He is a kind pastor and a brilliant preacher. I answered him by saying that I am trying to come alongside people to share some things that I hope shift people's hearts about language for God. My argument, I hope, is more like how the poetry of the Psalms "argues" to trust God or the poetry of Emily Dickinson "argues" that the world is full of wonder. I hope what I offer opens your heart and feeds faith.

2 Fathers—Created Better and the Only Creators

Wives are cautioned not to take over the spiritual authority and responsibility of their husbands.
> —Lutheran Church—Missouri Synod, "The Creator's Tapestry"

My dear boy, no woman is a genius. Women are a decorative sex. They never have anything to say, but they say it charmingly. Women represent the triumph of matter over mind, just as men represent the triumph of mind over morals.
> —Oscar Wilde, *The Picture of Dorian Gray*

What we think about people influences what we think about God—and vice versa. Another way to say this is that understanding God as Father and Jesus Christ as the Son of the Father has a context, one that reaches back into ancient history and the ways people assigned status to people and meanings to bodies. In this chapter, I explore the ancient ideas that males were created better than all other humans and that fathers were the only ones who could legitimately create, which served to reinforce a male-identified God. The other half of these views meant females were inferior humans who could not legitimately create people, ideas, or societies. These beliefs were about power, and they influenced the Scriptures and therefore how to understand God. To get at how a male-identified God seemed normal, we need to dive into this history of sex and gender and power. Your own experiences might help you think about the meanings humans give to one another that are enmeshed with power.

When was the first time you realized other people gave meanings to your body? I was four years old. A family with two boys was visiting. It must have been warm because I remember I had on shorts. Before I put on my shirt, someone knocked on my door, so I opened it, bare chested. One of the boys was at the door and, upon seeing me, screeched, "I saw a girl's titties!" I didn't know what "titties" were, but because he seemed ridiculous, I slammed the door in his face.

Some months later, it was winter, and my little brother and I were staying with family friends who had three boys—one older, one about my age, and one a bit younger. We were sitting on a brown rug playing something, maybe rolling a ball around, when one of them shot his gun with suction-cup darts directly into my open crotch. They roared.

One part of my body was to yell about, another part was to shoot. Meaning. Others give meanings to bodies, sometimes meanings that we know are untrue or harmful, maybe even ridiculous.

The boys who gave me messages about my body likely did not make these messages up on their own. They absorbed them from others. I'm guessing people have given you messages about your body too—not only about your sex or gender but also about skin color, hair, size, age, or abilities. All day, every day, all kinds of people give messages to others about their bodies, yours and mine included.

These experiences are not limited to childhood for most of us. Messages about embodiment are often connected with power. Sometimes the messages are about controlling females. Controlling female bodies is sometimes about covering bodies up. Only thirty-one of the fifty US states—plus Washington, DC; Puerto Rico; and the Virgin Islands—have laws that protect nursing mothers from public indecency laws. Some states only passed these laws that protect nursing mothers as recently as 2008.[1] Controlling female bodies is sometimes about restricting what they look like. Schools and employers use policies and coercion to try to control Black persons' hair. For example, students are suspended or sent away in some schools and employees have their shifts withheld at certain companies if they wear their hair in dreadlocks.[2] The message is that female bodies and Black bodies need to be curbed and kept under control.

Sometimes the messages are about dismissing embodied female knowledge and experiences. Sometimes it is lethal. From 2006 to 2017, Black women with at least a college degree died at over five times the rate white women did after childbirth.[3] Many of these postpartum deaths are preventable, but Black women in the United States often die because medical practitioners do not always take their self-described pain and discomfort seriously.[4] The message is that some people are not trustworthy sources of information because of their bodies. It is as if female and Black and brown embodiment means these persons are not trustworthy for knowledge, insight, experience, ideas, and leadership.

But why does North American culture function this way? We all live with many worldviews about bodies. Through our worldviews, we understand "the way things are" and the way we want things to be. In the United States, we live within an inherited worldview that females are inferior. Humans often make up "rules" about how we should live our lives based on worldviews. So if the worldview is that females are inferior, the "rules" include controlling and distrusting females, as statistics and experience show. Whether we like them or fight them, the worldviews and the "rules" influence how we live.

History shows that power dynamics have governed "rules" about sex and gender and race for centuries. In the history of sex and gender that most significantly affects the United States, power has been ascribed to males, specifically to fathers. Idealizing males affects all ethnicities and cultures in the United States—and worldwide.[5] The intersection of sex and race theories[6] in this history puts the white father ahead of all other people, which influenced ideas about God and Jesus. Talking about this history matters for faith because this history of sex and gender and its intersection with race illuminate ancient and contemporary language and images for God. In this sprawling history, the power granted to men affects ordinary and holy language.

Understanding the legacy of how sex (not sexuality) was defined a very long time ago also makes clear some of the different messages about sex and gender in the New Testament, which Christians have fought over for a long time. Knowing some of the history also illuminates how Martin Luther, despite the realities of his time, said and did some radical things, all of which contribute to a Lutheran perspective on language and images for God that is multigendered. For now, we will look at the history of sex.

From ancient Greece (ca. 400 BCE) into the 1700s CE, one basic story was of primary influence. In places such as France, Germany, and England, people largely thought we had one-sex bodies—that is, all humans were various versions of the perfect human body, the male body. Beginning in the 1700s, as I explain in the next chapter, this understanding shifted gradually, and eventually people in these parts of Europe and their colonies largely thought of humans as being two sexes that were complete opposites. In essence, there is a one-sex worldview and there is a two-sex worldview, one very old and one rather new. In neither of these worldviews would my girl-child body be considered equal to or as legitimate as a boy-child. Instead, power, authority, and legitimacy in both one-sex and two-sex worldviews belong to men, particularly fathers.

Males Are Created Better

The one-sex model or worldview described above prevailed for centuries. Though they did not agree about everything relating to bodies, influential philosophers Hippocrates (ca. 460–ca. 370 BCE) and Aristotle (384–322 BCE) and the physician Galen (ca. 130–ca. 200 CE) thought about humans in ways that reflected a one-sex worldview. One common agreement among them was that males were better than females. A one-sex worldview was still the predominant way to understand humans in parts of Europe during the Protestant Reformation.[7]

To put these dates into perspective, from around the time of the prophets Ezra and Nehemiah in ancient Israel until the century Bach lived in Germany and Sojourner Truth was born during the rise of slavery in the United States, people generally thought all bodies were one "kind." There were no predominant ideas about "opposite sexes" like we have now. Bodies were generally understood, instead, as different in their degree of perfection. Think about this through the metaphor of cars. Automakers often make one kind of car but in different degrees, like luxury and standard models. In the one-sex model, men were the luxury sedans. Women were the standard sedans. Both are sedans; they are the same kind of car, but one is superior to the other. One is "more car" than the other. The best human—the fullest expression of human form and human life—was a man. Differences people detected in women meant they were imperfect versions of the "canonical" male body.[8]

Why did people think this way? For a long time, people relied on cosmic metaphysics for their knowledge. This meant people thought the universe was ordered from the heavens at the top of a hierarchy to a grain of sand below. God was highest, then the angels and archangels. Humans came next, but men were superior to all other people. Then came animals and plants, on down to grains of sand. Illustrations from different centuries depict this worldview of a cosmic hierarchy from high to low, sometimes with God the Father as a white man with a beard at the top. In this worldview, everything existed in a hierarchy of power and value. Human bodies, the thinking went, reflected the cosmic order and also went from high to low.

While perhaps slightly confusing, they did not think that how to understand sex came from *bodies*. Instead, the meaning of sex came from the cosmic hierarchy. As historian Thomas Laqueur puts it, sex during this very long era was "a social rank."[9] In other words, being a "real man" came from the cosmic order. Being a man was not based so much on your body; instead, men's power and privilege came from the universe. But only some males were "real men." For instance, you were a "real man" in ancient Greece if you were a citizen and had property, including wives, children, slaves, and land. Not all *males* in ancient Greece, however, were citizens because being a citizen depended on ethnicity and property ownership. Supposedly, bodies reflected the hierarchical order of all reality that God (or the gods) created. Already here is an indication of why God might be identified as male. If God has the most power, then God must be male identified. If God is at the top of a hierarchy and men were higher than women, then God must be masculine.

Beliefs Influenced How to Understand Bodies

This belief system about an order of the universe influenced how to understand bodies. Intellectuals and medical practitioners alike applied their conviction that females were imperfect males. This influenced how they understood reproductive organs, sexual pleasure, bodily fluids, and reproduction.

It is important to note this connection more generally: What we believe influences how we understand. These four examples from a one-sex worldview help illustrate how the belief that bodies were all "one kind" but in a hierarchy of power and value led to understanding that females were subsumed by males—or even invisible in a sense.

In a one-sex worldview, females mirror males—specifically, female sex organs imperfectly reflect male sex organs. This inverse view of bodies is often referred to as a homologue. Doctors in parts of Europe in the 1600s relied on stunning illustrations of female genitals and reproductive organs as male—but inside out.[10]

This male-centered view of female biology meant there was not even a common vocabulary in Latin, Greek, or European tongues for "vagina" until the seventeenth century. Similarly, ovaries were referred to with words for "testes" until into the 1700s.[11] The assumptions about humans having a single kind of body were so strong that apparently no one in Europe drew a female skeleton for medical training until 1759.[12] For hundreds of years, females were subsumed in male identity.

Just as the organs of the body were seen as "one kind" in a one-sex model of humans, sexual pleasure was too. The thinking was that since males have orgasms to reproduce, females must also have orgasms in order to receive the seed of a male. However, even pleasure was in a hierarchy. Males had better pleasure, it was generally understood.[13]

Another characteristic of thinking humans had "one kind" of body is that people thought there was one system of bodily fluids, like blood, milk, semen, and discharges. All these liquids, the thinking went, were related: Blood was changed to milk, and all people bled, could give milk, and had discharges of semen.[14] But fluids had different degrees of power. Bodies high in the hierarchy had strong fluids. Bodies low in the hierarchy had weak fluids. The fluids all mattered, but some were better than others.[15]

As the perfect degree of humanity, with the best bodies, pleasure, and fluids, men in a one-sex model were said to be solely responsible for reproductive generativity. The thinking was that men alone created. Reproduction was about power, not necessarily about biology. For example, Aristotle thought the female provided the body for a baby and the male provided the soul.[16] Providing the soul involved the male having an idea, a concept, that is gestated in the body of the female.[17] The male was giving power—not *actual* seed—to the female to house. Men were literally the source of all life and all ideas.

What this all means is that a one-sex body with two versions, as Laqueur writes, "was framed in antiquity to valorize the extraordinary cultural asser-tion of patriarchy."[18] Sex was a position or place taken, not a biological "fact." Your sex was your status. Your status was your sex, and it came from the belief in a metaphysical hierarchy of value and power.[19] Sex was about the making, meaning, and maintenance of power.[20] Androcentric language and images for God make sense in such a worldview because if, according to this worldview, males were so high in value, so powerful, and therefore the best, God must be too. Even the arguments of recent theologians against female-identified or feminine language for God display this kind of assumption that females are subsumed by males.

Only Fathers Legitimately Create

The power assigned to people was connected to claims about fatherhood.[21] To understand fathers in a one-sex model, let's go back to ancient Greece. As Laqueur writes, "To Aristotle being male *meant* the capacity to supply the sensitive soul without which 'it is impossible for face, hand, flesh, or any other part to exist.'"[22] In a one-sex worldview, the father is the creator of all, the only one who generates life and civilization. The only true parent is the father.

Only the man is the true parent because he has the "seed" (the power) that produces *legitimate* children, heirs. The woman does not contribute to a *legitimate* heir. *Illegitimate* children were thought to spring from the genitals of the female.[23] Fatherhood was about power.[24] In short, a one-sex model revered the father as the originator of legitimate heirs, the founder of civ-ilization and order, and the source of life.[25] Sex-based power showed up in language.

Aristotle used words to show this power of the father, of a "true" man. He correlated not only the power to create another human but also the power to produce ideas and the power to be a citizen—to be rational and to govern—with male seed. He went on to explain that *kurios* (master, lord, or owner in Greek) is the strength or power associated with male seed. Aris-totle thought men created an analogy of the cosmic order of creation when they produced another person. Only men created another *legitimate* human, produced *legitimate* ideas, and were *legitimately* citizens—part of public life. And therefore the word *kurios* referred to men.

In contrast, Aristotle used the Greek word *akuros* to refer to having little or no political authority and/or capacity to create, whether humans, ideas, or public life. Tellingly, Aristotle used *akuros* for females and for boys.[26] Females and boys cannot create another legitimate human or legitimate ideas and cannot be legitimate citizens. They cannot be part of public life. In essence, Aristotle connects the power to create with the power to speak with authority. They are both associated with male seed. And therefore, with men. Only fathers legitimately create anything that is legitimate.

Briefly consider some of the connections to God, whom Christians confess as the source of all creation. For example, the Christian tradition has revered God the Father and focuses on masculine identity for God. Because people thought only fathers legitimately created other people, ideas, and society, it would have made sense to understand God as Father. Because people thought men were superior, it would have made sense to understand God as masculine. To make these connections does not deny God's power. But it becomes easier to see how God's power is interpreted through a particular worldview.

Women Are Worse and Cannot Legitimately Create

Women in a one-sex worldview are in some ways illegitimate. Scholar of classics Mary Beard argues that "looking harder at Greece and Rome helps us to look harder at ourselves, and to understand better how we have learned to think as we do."[27] This could not be truer when trying to unravel the meanings of human and divine fathers and sons, particularly in Christianity. Ancient views of women's speech tell part of the story.

Not only could women not legitimately create a person, but they could also not legitimately speak. Women who tried to speak were not legitimately women. We see examples of men telling women to be silent very early in written literature in Greece, as Beard points out, and this message would be repeated throughout history and Christianity.

In Homer's *Odyssey*, Telemachus, son of Penelope and Odysseus, orders Penelope silent and sends her to her room. This nearly three-thousand-year-old story was just the beginning of a long line of such stories, with only a few exceptions,[28] that narrate the necessity of women's silence and the outrageousness of their attempts to speak with authority. As Beard is careful to note, the stories do not simply disallow women public speech. Instead, they show that public speech was an attribute of being a man. If a woman spoke in public, she was not a woman.[29] This is an example of how sex was (a) status. Any woman who tried to claim public speech was considered aberrant.[30] Women who spoke went against their rank. Men in their superior rank possessed the authority to speak, create, kill, and rule. They made civilization happen.[31]

Hundreds of years after Homer wrote about Telemachus silencing and restricting Penelope, Aristotle and Plutarch reinforced the worldview that women are worse than men and cannot legitimately create. Aristotle (384–322 BCE) thought that the female mind and uterus awaited the male "active principle."[32] He argued that if women had seed equal in power to men's, they would inseminate themselves.[33] Since women aren't doing this, their seed is weak; it is illegitimate. Seed and intellect are intertwined: women also have illegitimate thoughts, unless they are generated by men's ideas.

Plutarch (46–ca. 119 CE), a Greek philosopher much favored by Rome, traveled to some of the same places the apostle Paul did, such as Rome and Corinth. Plutarch echoes Aristotle by saying that it was incredibly important to protect society from women and women from themselves. Women, he said, needed to receive the proper seeds of men's ideas; otherwise, "they, left to themselves, conceive many untoward ideas and low designs and emotions."[34] A woman's uterus, mind, and voice needed to be governed by the legitimate "seed" of her husband.[35]

Greek and Roman mythology shows how terrible it is when women take power, furthering the idea that men are completely justified to maintain power.[36] One result of a one-sex worldview is that men have a duty to save civilization from women. From one angle, you could say that it was necessary for fathers to rule. Beard argues that these ancient perspectives continue to have a strong influence, including in the United States. I think the ancient rejection of females and what is labeled feminine also continues to have a strong influence on Christianity.

The Scriptures

Ancient views about sex influenced the Scriptures. Like some of the examples from a one-sex worldview, the Scriptures also often separate what is female or feminine from what is good, authoritative, creative, and divine. Not always, but often. For instance, in the Hebrew Bible, fathers and sons are generally the central characters of stories. In the New Testament, God is a father, Jesus is a son, and disciples are men. The Scriptures focus a lot on men because they were written primarily by men in a cultural context that favored maleness.

One result of this gender-based unevenness in the Bible is that the Christian tradition has focused more on the negative about females than the positive. For example, most Christians could probably recall the directions for women in parts of the New Testament—to be silent, to obey, not to teach men—but the Good Householder is rarely in chancels or lessons. So what can we observe in Scripture to aid us in recognizing inclusive language for God as scripturally, evangelically, and theologically faithful? Try to keep in mind my analogy of listening to music, because like listening for the baritone sax and percussion in a musical piece, the Scriptures also have patterns and themes that are not always noticed.

Although the image of God as father can be found in a few Psalms and is used a few times in the book of Isaiah, the Hebrew Bible has fewer explicit references to God as a father than does the New Testament. In the Gospel of Mark, which scholars think is the earliest written Gospel, Jesus calls out to God as Abba (Father or Daddy) one time, when he prays in desperation in the Garden of Gethsemane (Mark 14:36). The writer of Mark only gives an explicit reference to Jesus as Son of God four times, once from Jesus in a parable, twice from God's voice in the heavens, and once from the Roman soldier at the cross. However, the three later Gospels, Matthew, Luke, and John, crystallize and reinforce the father-son theology. It has become the way to understand the Triune God.

At the same time, the Scriptures are woven with the threads of resistance to androcentrism. God as the Father has a context. Galatians and 1 Timothy both wrestle with fatherhood. In the letter to the Galatians, Paul rejects the false fatherhood of Rome, New Testament scholar Brigitte Kahl explains. In the Roman Empire, Caesar was the "father of the fatherland." He was divine and ruled with sacred power. In ancient myths, political power brought salvation. The earth and its peoples were saved by divinely appointed kings, upon whom the cosmos depended to stem death-dealing chaos.[37] The ancient Middle East was familiar with this theme.

Caesar was one of those saviors. He embodied divine fatherhood through war, execution, and subjugation.[38] All nations conquered by Rome symbolically became one under Caesar Augustus, who by 2 BCE claimed the title *pater patriae*—the father of all households, government, and the world.[39] Here we see a one-sex model in a superlative expression. A father, who has the power to create people and the authority to rule people, is in charge. He not only stems chaos for nations but also produces peace and civilization. Caesar as pater patriae is thus the progenitor and guardian of the nation.

Caesar Augustus promotes himself with an ancient mythological image as the father who delivers the world from chaos. This includes conquering the descendants of an unruly people called "the Giants." We know them as the Galatians, recipients of Paul's ministry and the letter we have in Scripture. The Galatians under Augustus's rule become "the newborn or adopted 'sons'" of the Roman emperor.[40] Augustus became their new father by taking their territory, by becoming their ruler, and by forgiving them for their former chaos. He redeems them.

The Galatians then owe the father Caesar Augustus their worship because they have been adopted. They are now "sons of the universal imperial father and his fatherland."[41] The Galatians are reborn through Caesar's violence, through war and death, through defeat. They are resurrected as new creatures, sons of the father, to whom "they owe faith, loyalty, and worship."[42] Caesar Augustus is supposed to be the Galatian's father and God. It is *this* God whom the apostle Paul rejects in the letter to the Galatians.

Paul rejects the divinity and fatherhood of the emperor. When writing to the Galatians, for example, Paul, himself a Roman subject, does not acknowledge their new imperial identity as adopted sons of Rome. Instead, he claims the Galatians as heirs of Abraham (which is still a male lineage)—through Christ. The Galatians, Paul claims, are heirs not by bloodlines—and not by the fatherly power of the Roman emperor.[43] Against the emperor's assertion to have redeemed and rebirthed the Galatians, Paul claims that *Jesus Christ* redeems and rebirths.[44] Paul pitches a battle about who is the savior, arguing that those who belong to Christ are justified or saved not by the emperor and the law of imperial Rome but by Christ alone: "Knowing that a man [a person] is not justified [reckoned as righteous] by the works of the law, but by the faith of Jesus Christ" (Gal 2:16 KJV). The followers of Jesus declared that the Father of Jesus is the God of Israel, not Caesar. This was heresy and rebellion in the Roman Empire.

Other New Testament writers similarly reject the Roman emperor as divine father. In her study of power struggles in early Christianity, biblical scholar Elsa Tamez investigates the intersection of class, gender, and ethnicity in theological differences and leadership battles in 1 Timothy. The writer of 1 Timothy, Tamez argues, uses titles like *father* and *savior* to evangelize and to declare which god to trust.[45] Like Galatians, 1 Timothy rejects the Roman emperor as father and savior, as paterfamilias, in favor of the God of Jesus Christ as Father.[46] Timothy also rejects the emperor as an epiphany or divine incarnation. Instead, Jesus Christ is the true epiphany. Like the Galatians, this community also rejects the emperor, a risky confession in a world rife with the traditions of worshipping a god or a ruler who creates new life through violence.[47] Instead, Jesus is the savior. God is the (true) Father.

Although both Galatians and 1 Timothy reject the fatherhood and divinity of Caesar Augustus, the writer of 1 Timothy encourages the community to whom he is writing to live within the social structures of Roman fatherhood. This means Caesar Augustus should be their example.[48] Caesar declared himself father of the fatherland—pater patriae. The analogous model for families is paterfamilias—father of the family. The writer of 1 Timothy, then, is encouraging people to live in Christian community in similar gendered power relations to the patriarchal household of the Roman Empire. Tamez points out four central values 1 Timothy encourages: dependence, subordination, strict gender roles, and obedience. They echo Roman culture.

In the patriarchal family, the father is head not only of his "own" bloodline but also of the entire household (wife, children, other children, servants, slaves, and beneficiaries). He owns the land and the people. They depended on him and were subordinated to him.[49] This is a vertical view of family and government. The father is the keeper of order and the giver of life. The king is responsible for protecting subjects and demanding obedience.[50]

Family and social structures, particularly of the aristocracy, depended on strict gender roles.[51] Tight control of lineage and households protected wealth. Gender-based dependence, subordination, and obedience were so important that Augustus implemented a law that women had to be obedient to male householders and marry and have children.[52] Of course, there were rich women who had authority over children, slaves, and people indebted to the paterfamilias, but they remained under the authority of male heads.[53] Marriage and motherhood made women legitimate. We can see a one-sex worldview at work.

The central point here is that the writer of 1 Timothy appropriates the Roman imperial values for the community to survive. The writer of 1 Timothy encourages the community to act like Roman citizens—in a patriarchal order of dependence, subordination, strict gender roles, and obedience to the earthly father. Although the writer of 1 Timothy believes that only the heavenly Father is God, fatherhood on earth should mirror Caesar's relationship to conquered nations. This is a good example of the practical effects of a one-sex worldview on Scripture. Father is best. As I explain in chapter 4, Martin Luther repeats similar themes. It is worthwhile to note again that when the Scriptures and an influential theologian at times support a hierarchy of power and value based on sex and gender, it is easy to continue to imagine God in masculine language and images.

In contrast, Paul's letter to the Galatians is rife with imperial disruption across the board—in heaven and on earth. There was a kind of ordinariness to violent fatherhood in the Roman imperial context.[54] Under Caesar the father, redemption comes through violent conquest. In contrast, Paul proclaims a divine father who brings new creation through resurrection from the dead. Paul's proclamation not only rejects a divine father (Caesar) who rules by gender-based superiority and violence; it also rejects earthly fathers who act the same way.[55]

From my perspective, Paul's thoroughgoing rejection of the violent gender-based and ethnic-based model of divine fatherhood pushes the Galatians for mutuality and reciprocity in the earthly realm: "There is no longer Jew or Greek, there is no longer slave or free, there is no longer male and female; for all of you are one in Christ Jesus" (Gal 3:28). Indeed, there is no longer (male) self and subordinated, imperfect (female) other. Here is a *theological* glimmer of undoing father primacy. Calling upon the God of Jesus Christ as Father in Paul's context disrupts Roman imperial claims of divine masculinity like we find in a one-sex worldview. In Christ there is no longer high and low, legitimate and illegitimate among humans. And the title *Father* for God surfaces in the New Testament context as a rejection of male superiority.

Conclusion

In a one-sex worldview, sex was all about power and no power, legitimacy and illegitimacy, and authentic parenthood—fatherhood. Sex was intertwined as part and parcel with social and political systems. Men were better. Female bodies were in a sense invisible because there was no language for female anatomy.[56] Men had the most power. And not just any men, but citizens, householders, fathers. Legitimate men were fathers. And they needed sons. In contrast, women were not creators of life, ideas, or society.

Sex determined your station in life—your status.[57] Your station in life determined things like what clothing to wear. For example, even into the sixteenth century, you could not dress like a man if you weren't born with the privileges of a man. Because clothing signified status, for example, the same was true about furs. Sumptuary laws decreed only people of a certain class could wear furs. It was like this with clothing that was considered for men: someone could dress like a man only if they had *the right* to do so.[58]

Rules like this were in place not long before the start of the twenty-first century. Although pants on women were not consistently banned across the United States in the twentieth century, there were restrictions related to the "right" to wear pants. For example, in 1938, a trial witness was put in jail for five days because she refused to wear a dress to court.[59] Until 1993, the US Senate banned pants for women on the floor.[60] And until 2016, female British Airways flight attendants had to wear skirts.[61] The right to wear certain clothing is only one part of a larger matrix of the meanings and status we give to people. Status based on sex also determined if your public voice was legitimate.

Stations in life that are determined by sex and gender influence language and images for God. When the power to create belongs only to men and when females are subsumed by males or are nearly invisible, we need to consider the influence on language and images for God. As Christians, we confess that God is the source of all creation. We confess that God is the source of all power and might in Genesis every year in Advent lessons, and we sing it weekly through the Psalter. Then in the New Testament, according to the Gospel of John, God created through speaking a word, an idea. And in Roman-occupied Palestine, when New Testament texts were written, God is overwhelmingly confessed as Father.

If public speech belongs only to men and if a woman who speaks publicly is out of order, aberrant, and not really a woman, then it doesn't even seem possible that God could be associated with the feminine or what is female identified. In the universe of a one-sex body, God-She is not a legitimate God. When the worldview is all about fathers and sons, Beard's challenge starts to make some sense. She observes, "You cannot easily fit women into a structure that is already coded as male; you have to change the structure."[62]

This is why Christians need generative conversations and faithful changes in language and images for God. If a referent to a male God is about power and legitimacy because of ancient concepts of fatherhood, we need theological renewal to talk about power and legitimacy—in a legitimate way. Dialogue might not be easy, but the ELCA has through its social statement on sexism committed itself to complex thinking, generous collaboration, and the proclamation of God's love.[63]

In the next chapter, we turn to a two-sex worldview, one that will seem far more familiar. Examining the ways a two-sex worldview and race theory intersect and reinforce each other explains more clearly why there are so many images of God the Father and Jesus as white men with beards. Keeping a two-sex worldview in mind will also allow us to discern how it lies behind some contemporary arguments against feminine language and images for God. Once we grasp more fully the recent history of sex and gender, we can begin to understand not only human but also divine language as multigendered.

3 Fathers—Ruling Sex and Ruling Race

In the name of liberation from male "domination," women must not appropriate to themselves male characteristics contrary to their own feminine "originality."

—Pope John Paul II, *Mulieris Dignitatem*

Judged by the evolving nineteenth-century ideology of femininity, which emphasized women's roles as nurturing mothers and gentle companions and housekeepers for their husbands, Black women were practically anomalies.

—Angela Y. Davis, *Women, Race, and Class*

In this chapter, I explore the ways scientists and philosophers beginning in the eighteenth century cultivated theories about opposite sexes and opposite races. Both of these ideas about people are at work in recent history and contemporary life. A two-sex worldview is also active in Christian teaching and faith and plays a significant role in arguments against feminine or female-identified language and images for God in favor of arguments that God's very being is masculine.

To begin, the story of voting rights illustrates how worldviews on sex and race were battlegrounds for power in the recent history of the twentieth century. People were fighting to establish who was "high" and who was "low" and who was legitimate and who was illegitimate. As you read, you might reflect on your own views about opposite sexes and different races. In what ways do you think your views about sex and gender and race and ethnicity influence how you understand and relate to the three persons of the Trinity?

When my grandmothers were young girls, women who said they wanted the right to vote were treated by many people as outrageous. They were supposedly acting against their "feminine nature." In 1917, white women who stood silently outside the White House to advocate for voting rights were put in prison. As the fight for the vote intensified and imprisonment became political, one woman had her wrists chained above her head to the cell door. One was put in a holding cell with men overnight. The guard who deposited her there told the men to do with her what they wanted.[1]

As women of many racialized identities actively campaigned to have the right to vote, white women were at odds with one another over the participation of Black women in the movement. White women and men regularly pushed Black women out of integrated public protests and organizing. During the first suffrage parade in Washington, DC, which was set to coincide with President Woodrow Wilson's inauguration, sections from various states and organizations were integrated. But some white women tried to keep Black women out of the Illinois delegation. Famed journalist and activist Ida B. Wells was targeted for removal. One white woman argued the delegation should act with "moral courage" and remain integrated in their work, including the parade. Wells responded to the debate in anger, saying, "If the Illinois women do not take a stand now in this great democratic parade then the colored women are lost."[2] Once the parade began, Wells slipped back into her place. But the power of white supremacy proved to be a potent threat to voting equality for Black and brown women.

Just as women were not united in their arguments about who was "good enough" to vote, men were also divided on the question of women's status. Men jeered and threatened other men who supported suffrage for women, calling them unmanly "pansies" and asking them where their skirts were. Public parades were a particularly vulnerable place for prosuffrage men.[3] Before running for president in 1884, Wilson described his attendance at the Association for the Advancement of Women in Baltimore in a letter to Ellen Louise Axson, whom he eventually married: "Barring the chilled, scandalized feeling that always overcomes me when I see and hear women speak in public, I derived a good deal of whimsical delight . . . from the proceedings."[4] Through prison guards, activists, and the president of the United States, sexism and racism shaped the nation, determining who is high and who is low, who speaks legitimately and who speaks illegitimately. Many claimed that women did not have legitimate rights to vote and to speak because they were too weak in body, mind, and spirit. In other words, a two-sex worldview meant that women were completely different from men and therefore less competent.

US history reveals many links between sex and race and violence and legitimacy. As only one of many examples, the federal government only first allowed American Indian people the right to vote in 1924. Yet at the same time, white men with power and influence put laws in place in Oklahoma so they could be custodians of American Indian women who held the rights to oil. The Osage women who held oil rights there were some of the richest people in the United States at the time. After gaining control of their oil rights and money, various white men systematically murdered some of them and their heirs to inherit their wealth.[5] The perpetrators were largely protected from prosecution, leaving the clear message that Osage women and their families should not legitimately have such wealth and the power that came with it. Whether American Indian, Black, or white—or Asian, Pacific Islander, or Latina—women of the early twentieth century lived with violence and other forms of retribution for speaking out or gaining political power. It did not end in the twentieth century, meaning that the intersecting ideas that women and racialized people are inferior to men and white people and that they are "less" legitimate influence church life.

About one hundred years after suffrage parades, nearly half of surveyed pastors and deacons who identify as women in the ELCA reported sexual harassment, compared to 13 percent reported by people who identify as men. The highest number of reported instances is in congregations.[6] Workplace sexual harassment is illegal in the United States, and yet women in ordained ministry experience lots of it by congregants, colleagues, community members, and others. In a similar vein, women from racialized communities are compensated on average below white women and all men.[7] Other church bodies with women in ordained ministry reported similar problems. My point is that the United States and the ELCA show enduring habits to assess people as "legitimate" or "illegitimate" based on sex and race and to punish or restrict persons who challenge the rules of such worldviews.

At the same time, the ELCA teaches that patriarchy and sexism are sins and tries to support equity and flourishing among all people. However, the national and global context of Christian teaching on sex and gender is to the contrary. From papal encyclicals to popular Christian teachings to other Lutheran views, many Christians hold firmly to the idea that there are only two completely opposite sexes and that women are secondary to men in power and status.[8] Such views hold enormous power over our collective imaginations regarding language and images for God.

Political Bodies: Defining Bodies with Power

Defining people as opposites based on anatomy is a relatively recent development in history, even though we may be accustomed to it. The tipping point in history came with scientific discovery, which exploded especially in parts of Europe in the 1700s and 1800s. For instance, researchers started to study cadavers. Science replaced cosmic metaphysics as the trusted source for knowledge. While science advanced lifesaving knowledge and techniques, it also became a tool of control.

During this era, people in parts of Europe and in many colonies were agitating for freedom from bondage. They argued for equality and shared privileges. Social upheavals were widespread: the French and American Revolutions, American Indian resistance, the Mexican-American War, rebellions against the British Empire (e.g., in India, Ireland, and the colonies), the rise of evangelical Christianity and industrialism, early entreaties to women's rights, and slaves' resistance to bondage in places such as England, Haiti, and the United States.

In these many agitations for freedom from bondage, some people in Europe and many colonies declared everyone had shared privileges, equality, and commonality. Imaginations and values were shifting toward seeing people as equals, even with their differences. When so many people began to fight for freedom based on inherent rights as equal humans, science historian Londa Schiebinger explains, the reaction was to find ways to prove that people were different, which they believed meant that some deserved to be treated as less important than others.[9] People were using science, the new source of knowledge, to justify inequalities. For instance, if inferiority by sex and race could be "proven" by science to be natural, who could possibly argue with it? The growing field of natural sciences[10] defined the foundation of the social order. Bodies became the foundation, the root, of political meanings and the foundation of gender and race.

Through science, people searched for and highlighted differences between men and women, and they created another model that just happened to reinforce another hierarchy of power, value, and authority based on sex and gender and race. While some anthropologists at the time argued that there were too many variations within groups of people and it was therefore silly to classify people, most researchers did so and came up with a variety of distinct classifications of people.

When power plays a role in interpreting human bodies, philosopher Michel Foucault calls it "political anatomy."[11] As we will see, bodies became remarkably political when people argued for equality. And although the era over battles for women specifically to have the right to vote and against slavery may seem a long time ago, in the twenty-first century, we still live with the inherited worldviews that people are created only in opposite sexes and in a hierarchy of race and ethnicity.

The Sex Binary

Getting to the point of thinking that people are complete opposites based on bodies did not happen overnight.[12] If you recall, in a one-sex worldview, people were created along a hierarchy with God at the top, followed by angels, then men, then women, on down to the grains of sand. In a one-sex worldview, people are all one kind of human, but men are the perfect version.

In contrast, in a two-sex worldview, people are two totally different kinds of humans, one side of a binary or another, but men are still the best kind.[13] Humans are said to have opposite bodies, character, thinking, abilities, and vocations. The binary is especially vivid in Christian teachings about men and women being complementary. In complementarianism, as it is called, the belief is that God created two opposite sexes and genders. According to this view, men are rational, and women are emotional; men lead, and women follow or obey. Many Christian churches teach this view. For some, this is bondage. To return to the metaphor of cars, in this worldview, men are Peterbilt semitrucks. Women are Honda Civics. Both are vehicles with many commonalities. But one is clearly superior in power.

They are both important, but they are built differently to serve very different purposes.

The "political anatomy" of women's bodies meant that women's physical, intellectual, and moral qualities were governed by power dynamics. In stark contrast to the "political anatomy" of Black slave women, whose bodies were ruled over but not idealized, white women's bodies were controlled and idealized to argue that women should not be in the public sphere. In the 1700s, parts of Europe panicked about falling birth rates, which meant greater national insecurity, so politicians linked motherhood to nation building. Countries that needed more babies supported the idea that women were the opposite of men and therefore should stay at home, have babies, and not vote. As early as 1707, Denmark so feared a decreased population that it passed a law authorizing young women to have babies inside and outside of marriage. Having babies outside of marriage was previously scandalous. Now they had a law to support it.

As that century unfolded further, Germany and France passed laws that idealized the mother's breast. In both countries, doctors advocated laws to force healthy mothers to nurse their babies. In the midst of the French Revolution, with its heady calls for equality and its disruption of class privilege, delegates to the French National Convention lifted up the female breast as the proof "from nature" that women cannot be citizens or have public power.[14] Bodies became the explanation for status, vocation, and power.

European researchers also argued that bodies define character and morals. They described females as being passive for physical reasons. First, when researchers realized females could conceive without physical pleasure, they defined females as passive in sexuality.[15] Second, researchers discovered the female egg. In a positive light, people came to realize that females contribute to pregnancy. But because researchers realized ovulation usually happens without female action or knowledge, they defined females as passive in reproduction. Researchers rooted female identity, previously grounded in cosmic metaphysics, in the body itself.

Because women were identified as passive,[16] men argued that women should neither be part of public life, nor tell men what to do, nor even ride bicycles. They needed to wear skirts and stay in their place. Some doctors reinforced the ideal of female passivity by anesthetizing wives for their husbands to make them pregnant. Women's public and personal lives were supposed to be passive. Suddenly, as never before, there were texts that argued for biological bases for human moral order.

Scientists' assumptions about female passivity influenced how they interpreted what they were learning. Discovering the female egg was radical; it meant that males might not be the sole creator of humankind. One anatomist wrote in 1737 that the discovery of the egg might have taken "much from the dignity of the male sex."[17] However, because someone else discovered sperm were active in semen, "by this Noble Discovery, [he] at once removed that Difficulty."[18] Scientists then "concluded" that the egg was passive, that it was a harbor for the very active sperm to create a child because they expected to find female passivity. Eggs "must" be passive because females are. Sperm "must" create the child because men are the creators.[19]

Some of these discoveries about human differences were good, of course, but much of the scientific world in Northern Europe became obsessed with finding differences everywhere they could to justify female inferiority and obedience. People began to think cells, bodies, and social roles were all interrelated—and that these were all female-male opposites. As one biologist of the time said, "What was decided among the prehistoric Protozoan cannot be annulled by an act of Parliament."[20] He characterized a predominant view that bodies *were* the meaning of human lives. And thus women were not legitimate citizens because of their bodies. Once again, if science was "proving" the inferiority of females, there is little room for a female-identified God.

The Race Hierarchy

During the same era, "scientific" theories about race became yet another way to declare that some people are not legitimate because of their bodies. Theories about sex were related to theories about race.[21] Just as many researchers and interpreters looked for differences between females and males, they looked for differences between Africans and Europeans.

By the middle of the 1700s, some influential biologists argued that skeletons and skulls told the truth about race-based moral and intellectual superiority.[22] Language started to match the political anatomy of that era. In a publication in 1795, anatomist and anthropologist Johann Blumenbach first published the word *Caucasian* to refer to the best of humanity. He made this term up based on the people of the Caucasus mountains, people he thought were the most beautiful and who he thought were likely the original humans.[23]

One strange way in which sex and race anatomy intersected in that era had to do with the beard. Throughout written history, the beard has been revered (or not) in various times and by various cultures. For example, the ancient Egyptians thought it was a sign of virility and therefore leadership. The only woman in addition to Cleopatra VII to rule ancient Egypt by herself, Hatshepsut, was so capable that people gave her the symbol of kingship: not a crown but a beard. Beards were also a symbol of ruling manliness in many parts of Europe in the 1600s. From Greece to France to Germany, stiff penalties came for damaging a man's beard or even plucking a whisker. Because a man's beard was traditionally connected with virility, strength, and masculinity, cutting it was a form of punishment and subordination. Cutting anyone's hair was also a form of punishment and subordination.[24]

Beards became a symbol of racial superiority as these theories about sex and race were developing. Carl Linnaeus, famous for classifying plants and animals, said in a lecture in 1740, "God gave men beards for ornaments and to distinguish them from women."[25] By 1786, yet more natural historians assigned intellect and morals to beards. The "white" race, it was said, had the best beards. Indigenous peoples of the Americas were assessed as inferior because they were thought to be beardless. One naturalist wrote that they were inferior people due to "the want of one very characteristic mark of the sex, to wit, that of a beard."[26] Black and brown men were supposedly not legitimate compared to white men with beards.

Beardless men were not good people and were basically subhuman. Women, who are typically beardless, also lacked strength and good moral character.[27] But women just did not need beards, philosopher of religion Immanuel Kant reasoned, because women are subject to men. For example, late in the 1700s, he fumed about a few learned women and wrote that they "might just as well have a beard, for that expresses in a more recognizable form the profundity for which she strives."[28] Kant was Lutheran.

In this worldview of political anatomy, God therefore *had* to be white and male, signified by a beard. If you look for artwork of God online, much of it shows God as a white man with flowing white hair and a beard, sitting in the heavens. And if you look for artwork of Jesus Christ online, much of it also

Figure 3.1. *God the Father,* 1885–96. Viktor Mikhaylovich Vasnetsov (1848–1926). Found in the collection of the State Tretyakov Gallery, Moscow. Heritage Image Partnership Ltf / Alamy Stock Photo.

shows Jesus as a white man with a beard. According to the thinking about sex and race in that era, science "proved" that God the Father and Jesus deserved beards and were white.

Sex and Race: A Hierarchy of Women

People also defined power based on "races" of women. A hierarchy of women was yet another form of *political anatomy.* To determine which women were "the most" human, researchers looked at menstrual blood, breasts, and genitalia. The old assumption was that beards and menstrual blood came from excess bodily fluids, which made someone a superior human. Just like they thought Indigenous men did not have beards, naturalists declared that Indigenous women did not menstruate.[29] Some researchers thought European women were "more" human because they supposedly had heavier menstruation than other women and apes.[30] They gave little regard to factors like trauma and stress, natural medicines, or their sheer lack of access to studying all women's bodies accurately.

Breasts were also a standard. Artists, authors, and scientists idealized and idolized European women's breasts in literature, artwork, and science. The North European standard for quintessential breasts was firm and spherical, which they thought was a sign of moral superiority. Naturalists from Europe often characterized African women's breasts as so large and droopy that they could sling them over their shoulders.[31] Droopy breasts, they thought, were a sign of moral inferiority.

Naturalists were also obsessed with studying African women's genitalia, which they characterized as inferior to white women's genitalia. They turned the results of their observations and imaginations into sexual character and morality.[32] European scientists thought African women were sexually promiscuous and unruly. They were not "legitimate" women.

In this worldview of political anatomy, God could never be a Black woman. Womanist Christian theologians have been pushing back on this legacy for decades. These Black and brown women teach, preach, and write from the perspective of being doubly marginalized in the Christian tradition. They reach back into the Black church tradition and forward as women to preach the good news that they are beloved, despite the legacy of white supremacy. The legacy of racism influences not only self-worth but images of God. Womanist theologian Karen Baker-Fletcher writes, "We [Black women] cannot love God if we refuse to love what God loves, and God loves us. If God does not identify with black women, then what kind of God is that?"[33] God, she reasons, identifies with all of humanity, no matter our skin color or ethnicity, and God identifies with all sexes because Jesus was made from dust, just as every single human is. This is God *for us*.

Science, history proves, can be biased. People can develop harmful theories and practices supposedly based on science that are racist and patriarchal. Where does this leave us? It leaves us with questions about power. In the theories of race, white men have power because they are not Black and brown men, and white women have power because they are not Black and brown women. In a two-sex worldview, men have power because they are not women. Said another way, men are men because they are not women. In this two-sex worldview, fathers are believed to divert chaos and create order. Fathers in the last several centuries continue to hold significant power, especially in our collective imaginations. Some cultural messages from the last hundred years further underscore the power we assign to fathers, whether earthly or heavenly.

Fathers and Sons: An Ideal of Patriarchy

Although fathers are no longer considered solo creators, in many ways, they remain in charge and idolized in a two-sex worldview. In the twentieth century, fathers continued to be considered the best and the highest. There is the idea that they avert chaos. In a two-sex model, the father is primary because he is biologically distinct from the mother; he is opposite to her supposed passivity, softness, and weakness. He therefore must be the head of the family and rule social and religious life, so the thinking goes, because he is different in his very being. In addition, the father is responsible for maintaining a sex binary. The idea that males and females are complete opposites and different in their very beings is a key argument against feminine language for God. The power and authority of fathers and social ideals about them in the United States affect Christian language and images for God—and our reactions to language for God that uses multiple genders. To understand what I am saying, it is worth considering messages about fathers in recent US history.

The idea of opposite sexes and the power fathers have probably affected your life. After World War II, there was a lot of anxiety about gender identity, especially in the white world. This anxiety about gender roles was wound into international politics. National security, the thinking went, depended on men acting like men and women acting like women.

This worked two ways, commentators believed. On the one hand, having "traditional" family structures and gender roles would make a country strong enough to ward off communism and nuclear threat. On the other hand, nuclear fallout or a communist society would cause chaos. A Harvard physician said in 1951 that nuclear war would open "the potential for sexual chaos."[34] Only the steady hand of the father in the correct place in the gender-based hierarchy could avert chaos.[35] The country was said to need manly men in order to be safe, a loud echo of ancient fears of chaos when women speak and have power. No wonder a female-identified God has seemed unacceptable.

After World War II, white women were told to return to their "natural" roles as wives and mothers. These roles apparently did not require intellectual skill because women were supposedly different in their very beings from men. For example, in 1957, *Ladies' Home Journal* published an article called "Is College Education Wasted on Women?" Possibly, the author writes. College is a means to an end for women—a husband. College education, it was said in popular literature, serves women no personal gain, for "certainly the happiest women have never found the secret of their happiness in books or lectures. They do the right thing instinctively."[36] Women's happiness, another popular advice magazine declared at the time, lay in supporting and encouraging her husband in *his* gender-specific role of breadwinner and husband.[37] "She" was supposed to live for "he." What *Ladies' Home Journal* published in 1957 echoed European parliaments in the eighteenth and nineteenth centuries. Women were not equal to men, and fathers and sons mattered the most.

Part of the man's role was to be a father who raised manly sons. In popular literature, sons who are anything like daughters were not allowed. For instance, an article in 1950 in *Better Homes and Gardens* asks, "Are we staking our future on a crop of sissies? . . . You have a horror of seeing your son a pantywaist, but he won't get red-blooded and self reliance [*sic*] if you leave the whole job of making a he-man of him to his mother."[38] As social biologist Anne Fausto-Sterling remarks, "Fatherhood itself became a new badge of manliness."[39] And fathers needed to do all they could to make sure sons were not like their mothers.

Maybe you grew up with these messages about mothers and fathers—and sons—and invisible daughters. Maybe you have thought about the effects on yourself. My mom entered university in 1957. A Lutheran pastor helped her be the first of her family to go to college, despite the prevailing view that she would not find fulfillment in using her mind. No matter when we were born, our collective and individual lives are influenced by these values and ideas about the sex binary and the role of fathers.

Feminist activist and scholar John Stoltenberg explores the connection between fathers and a fear of "pantywaist" sons in an essay that is not explicitly personal but clearly full of sorrow and regret. Fathers, Stoltenberg writes, are owners. Like the historians who explain that fathers owned people, land, and labor in both ancient and more recent eras, Stoltenberg detects similar ownership from roughly the 1950s to 1980s. "Adult men," he writes, "are entitled to ownership of every body that is birthed and every body that births."[40] Laws and culture, he points out, support what he calls "father right"—the right to *have* others and the right to be right. Fathers rule.

Policies and laws in the 1950s and 1960s supported father right. When my mom had her first teaching job after earning her university degree, she lived with friends, had a car, and paid for her own expenses. But the bank required her dad, who lived two thousand miles away, to cosign for her to get a credit card. In addition to ruling economics based on gender, the law ruled bodies based on gender. Only in 1965 did the US Supreme Court rule that it was legal for married persons to have access to birth control, and only in 1972 did it rule that it was legal for unmarried persons to have access to birth control. These are father rights.

The idea that fathers have rights over women and children seems to extend beyond the household. Think about the recent public cases of well-known Christian men (some pastors and politicians) who seemed to think they could "take" the women or children they wanted—and get away with it. Think about the headline news of athletes and coaches who do the same, from college football players to professional baseball players to Olympic team coaches and doctors. Father right allows violence.

The overarching problem, Stoltenberg thinks, is the way we bank every corner of our collective imaginations in father-right relationships, thinking that we are being religiously faithful or simply doing the right thing because this is the way things are.[41] Maybe we have done the same thing with masculine language for God.

The inherited idea that the father is in charge is personally devastating too. Although Stoltenberg writes in a generalized way about the father's rage and a son's attempt to find the father's love, I perceive Stoltenberg's sorrow over a deep separation from who he could have been. The father's anger, he writes, displaces sons from themselves, and he reflects on the ways the father rages against the son, the child who does not understand the anger or the rules that he apparently broke. Nearly five hundred years earlier, as I will show in the next chapter, Martin Luther struggled with his father's anger too. Both men's experiences are examples of the ways the ideas about fathers permeate how we understand ourselves and God. As Stoltenberg further describes, the son eventually realizes that he belongs to—is owned by—the father. The father will shape the son—and it will be an identity "defined against the mother."[42]

Some recent arguments against feminine and female-identified language and images for God appear to reflect these three values about fathers in a two-sex worldview that I have sketched out with commentary and examples from recent history. Fathers avert chaos. Fathers are inherently different from mothers in body, mind, and spirit. And fathers rule over or own others.

Although a few Lutheran theologians are among the most vocal opponents to feminine language for God, Robert Jenson's argument against gender-inclusive language for God seems to hover in the depths of every argument I have read against it, either explicitly or implicitly. He is worth quoting at length because we need to understand what is at stake: "'Father' was Jesus' peculiar address to the particular transcendence over against whom he lived. Just by this address he qualified himself as 'the Son.' . . . 'Spirit' was the term provided by the whole biblical theology for what comes of such a meeting between this God and a special human of his. . . . Emerging consciousness of the historic oppression of women rightly watches for expressions thereof also, or perhaps principally, in inherited interpretations of God. When such are found, Christianity has every reason to eliminate them. . . . Trinitarian Father-language cannot, however, be one such."[43] So far, Jenson's argument is that because Jesus called God Father in the Gospels, he showed that he was the Son. Jenson is also saying that the relationship between father and son is central to knowing the God of Jesus. Although Christianity should be wary of sexist oppression, he continues, language for God is one part of faith that cannot be assessed for the way male-focused language developed or the ways it affects Christian theology and the life of faith. From my perspective, the historical context of language and images for God matters enormously. We have seen how powerful the father-son ideals are—and how costly they are, not only to all others, but to fathers and sons themselves. Insisting on androcentric language appears to be an implicit sign of holding on to the father ruler who averts chaos. However, Jenson's explicit argument is ontological—that is, about the being of males and females.

Jenson relies on the two-sex worldview I have described to make his argument about language for God. He appears to be rooted in the perspective that men are men because they are not women—and that God is Father because he is not she, writing,

The choice between "mother" and "father," as terms of filial address to God, was and must be made according to which term is more easily separable from the reproductive role.

Sexuality, as the union of sensuality and differentiated reproductive roles and apparatus, is the glory of our specific humanity. . . . Within the mutuality of male and female, the female is ontologically superior. She is the more ineradicably human, for while sensuality and reproduction can socially be ripped apart in the male, . . . not even abortion can do this to the female. . . .

It is just the ontological inferiority of the male that offers "Father" rather than "Mother" as the proper term of address to Israel's sexually transcendent God, when a filial term is needed.[44]

Like the anatomists and interpreters beginning in the 1700s and like the magazine writers in the twentieth century, Jenson assigns human identities to reproductive roles—to our bodies.[45] And then he makes an argument that females are actually superior—and that this is the root reason to avoid calling God our Mother.

The Lutheran tradition, however, teaches that humans are equal in creation, equal in sin, and equal in redemption, so his argument seems to cling to male parts, literally and linguistically.[46] Jenson is not the only Christian theologian to argue for exclusively masculine language for God, but what he says is striking when we consider the history of sex and the ways fathers and sons have been prioritized over all others for centuries.

In one sense, through all these stories, practices, habits, ideas, and beliefs that prioritize the father over all others, we cut ourselves off from one another and even live within a kind of violence. Culturally and personally, as Stoltenberg writes, "we are so beholden to the father that we have sacrificed and betrayed all mothers in his name."[47] I think this is costly. By faith, how do we imagine anything different from father right on earth—and even in heaven? I think this imagining begins by looking at Scripture.

Chickens and Roosters, Hens and Cocks: A New Rule, a New Image

One of the images Jesus uses for himself is a hen who desires to gather the children of Jerusalem under her wing. I like it. I'm not especially fond of chickens, but Jesus as a mother speaks to me. It might be because I am a mother, but it's more likely because of the image of a brood of soft-feathered chicks nestled safely under the mother hen.

When my brother Paul was around seven, someone gave him a chick. I don't know why. Being town kids, we had not touched such soft feathers on a live creature before. Paul was smitten. Tiny and luminous yellow, the bird was so vulnerable. And so lonely. Despite having water and food in the cozy shoebox my brother prepared, and despite his doting, gentle care for this sweet little creature, it chirped in seeming desperation. None of us could comfort the chick. After a few days, it died overnight in the summer heat.

Maybe it wasn't just the heat, though. Maybe it was because the chick wasn't where it needed to be, under the soft wings of its mother. Maybe the chick needed to feel its mother's heartbeat, its mother's feathers on her brow, and its mother's brooding sound. Maybe when a chick is under her mother's wings, the hen's sounds vibrate through the chick. Maybe the chick's death was all about need.

Maybe Jesus is saying he is all about our needs. Saint Anselm of Canterbury (1033–1109) wrote, "But you, Jesus. . . . Are you not that mother who, like a hen collects her chickens under her wing? Truly master, you are a mother."[48] Maybe Jesus is saying that even when we set our faces against her, she is all about our needs: "Jerusalem, Jerusalem, the city that kills the prophets and stones those who are sent to it! How often have I desired to gather your children together as a hen gathers her brood under her wings, and you were not willing!" (Matt 23:37). Something more is going on with Jesus as a hen, though.

Jesus is a chicken, and in one sense, as I will explain, Jesus *is* chicken. The female image is not random. Jesus as a hen only makes full sense in relation to the male cock, the rooster. Theologian Debbie Blue helpfully reminds us that the rooster is an enduring cross-cultural symbol of violent, competitive masculinity.[49] Cockfighting may go back to the sixth century BCE near Jerusalem, and it is still done in many countries, even though it is illegal in some places. The Romans loved it. "The fighting cock," writes Blue, "like the empire,

Figure 3.2. Mosaic of mother hen with chicks. From the altar of Dominus Flevit Church on the Mount of Olives. Wikimedia Commons / Fallaner. Reprinted CC BY-SA 4.0. Rendered in black and white.

championed machismo, took its enemies down through brute force, and displayed a vigorous ferocity."[50] The cock could have been Rome's mascot.

By 63 BCE, Rome had colonized Judea, the southern kingdom of ancient Israel, with brute force and then called their colonial occupation of ancient Israel and other nations "peace." During Passover, Rome would post extra soldiers in Jerusalem, the holy city teeming with more than usual travelers. When Jesus spent his last Passover with disciples there, the Roman-occupied city was exceptionally tense. Guards were everywhere and were even posted up on the temple walls, where they are said to have offended and riled the crowds. Herod was working furiously to contain the growing Jesus movement. Pontius Pilate was responsible for bolstering Rome's response to dissent and unrest.

Then there is Jesus, the hen, in stark contrast to Rome, the cock. Throughout the Gospels, Jesus keeps saying that his life will end in crucifixion (Matt 26:2). Peter in particular does not like the sound of this. When Jesus tells the disciples they will all desert him, Peter protests loudly, shouting his allegiance to Jesus: "Even though I must die with you, I will not deny you" (26:35). Not to be outdone by Peter, the rest of the disciples say the same thing. I can see their heads bobbing, as if in a cartoon.

While Jesus is tortured by the Roman roosters, Peter tries to hang out in a courtyard nearby. People recognize him, and after the third time people say he was with Jesus of Nazareth, Peter "began to curse, and he swore an oath, 'I do not know the man!' At that moment the cock crowed" (Matt 26:74). Peter betrays. The cock crows. Virile Rome appears to be victorious.

So in this cockfighting culture, Jesus says he is a hen, a chicken—a female. In a culture obsessed with male violence, Jesus backs away. A cock that backs away in a fight or clucks when injured is called a chicken by cockfighters. Breeders call a cock like this a "sissy" by saying "the mother's blood is show-ing."[51] Good cocks aren't "pantywaists."

Yet Jesus says he is like a hen—a mother who covers her vulnerable, soft chicks under her wings, even when they resist her ways, as Peter does. She holds us especially when we are lost or despondent, like my brother's chick. Jesus shows what a good chicken is—fearless, not from cockiness or ideal-ized virility, but from a willingness not to be violent in a culture of idealized violent masculinity. She shows that we can trust her. Here is Jesus, God incarnate, a common chicken—a female—*for us*. Jesus is the chicken who will not fight, who will not compete with the Roman roosters who were obsessed with the hierarchy of cockfights, the arena, and the empire.

What does this have to do with sex? I think it has a lot to say about the cockfighting culture in one-sex and two-sex worldviews. On the one hand, Jesus as hen disrupts the hierarchy of the one-sex worldview. To reveal God's nature, Jesus takes the place of the lowest, a female, a nonfighting bird that does not even soar. On the other hand, Jesus as hen disrupts the binary of the two-sex worldview. Jesus claims multiple gender identities. Amid humans grasping for the best place in a hierarchy, Jesus reveals the way of no hierarchy but with distinctly gendered images. I find this compelling. I think we have clues to the same in gendered language for God.

Conclusion

To summarize, in a one-sex worldview, sex was a social rank that came from the way people thought the universe was created in a descending order of power and value. Women were less legitimate humans because they were not men, thought to be the perfect humans. In a two-sex worldview, sex was described as part of a person's very being (what is called one's ontology) and drawn from what science said about bodies. Science was used to argue for better and worse people based on sex and race. Women and racialized people were said to be morally inferior. Neither worldview is accurate or equitable.

A common thread linking hundreds of years of history is the fact that some people are deemed legitimate, while others are not. These determinations happen in ancient metaphysics, science, and religion. As I have tried to show, most often the people who are "high" and "legitimate" are men and white people. Their voices and bodies are legitimate in public—as citizens, students, teachers, and leaders—and in preaching and presiding. Fathers in this long history are primary, and sons are necessary. This history illuminates the sheer idolatry of androcentrism we have inherited. Thinking that God creates and requires a sex and gender hierarchy and binary further emphasizes "father right" socially and theologically.

Both of these models about sex get in the way of people receiving the gospel because both worldviews influenced language and images for God. One way forward is to continue to pay attention to Scripture, especially focusing on patterns and themes that might not be the predominant way to understand biblical texts, just like listening to music with ears for nondominant patterns and themes allows us to experience music in new ways.

Another way forward is to take seriously the ongoing history of sex and gender, both in understanding ourselves as humans and in understanding the Triune God. A model of multiplicity in sex and gender reorders, reorients, relativizes, reinterprets, and frees us from the primary role of fathers culturally and theologically. We next turn to Luther's life and theology as a compass for orientation as we consider language and images for God of multiple genders. As we will see, Luther disrupts sex and gender rules of his time. He did this in his personal life, teaching, pastoral care, and theology. So can we.

4 Fathers and Sons, Sex and Empire
Reading Luther through Luther

Possibilities are all about God's grace.
—Beverly Wallace, "Hush! No More!"

What do you know about Martin Luther? More specifically, what do you know about what he said about men and women and boys and girls? In this chapter, I bring together some of the ways Luther challenged how people in his time understood and treated others based on sex and gender. To do this, it is helpful to take stock of my method. I think it is important to read Luther through Luther's own life and work. Here is what I mean by this.

Reading Luther can be at once exciting and maddening, even disturbing. His poisonous words against the Jews in his day were used to fuel hatred and violence against them. His writings likely inspired prejudice that led to the Holocaust. He minced no words for Muslims and theological opponents, especially the pope. It can be disturbing to read his diatribes and to realize how they contributed to division and violence. And how they sometimes still do.

Many Lutherans worldwide now read Luther through the lens of his late medieval and early modern context, not to excuse him but to understand him as a flawed and gifted theologian. What matters is reading Luther's work and his life through his own theological insights. Every generation can be in conversation with what he offers from the distant world of Europe in the 1500s. The Lutheran theological tradition therefore continues to grow. He had the first word in the Lutheran tradition but certainly not the last.

Being faithful to the insights of the Lutheran vein of the Protestant Reformation is less about simply following Luther's teachings and more about interpreting them anew for this time. And so we listen not only to Luther but to his many contemporary interpreters. Just as we read Luther through Luther to contextualize and limit the influence of his hateful speech on Jews, Muslims, and the pope, we can do the same when it comes to gender and androcentrism; he said things that are misogynistic and homophobic. Luther's historical context was a one-sex worldview. Not surprisingly, Luther repeats this worldview in various biblical interpretations and other writings. However, despite this worldview, he also disrupts the ethos of the one-sex worldview.

In this chapter, I show that reading Luther's theology in relation to his life helps us understand how language and images for God need to include multiple genders. As other people who study Luther have noticed, his vocations as husband, father, pastor, and teacher provide an orientation to faithfully embracing language and images for God from all genders. First, we turn to examples from what Luther said and did regarding marriage, education, pastoral care, and inheritance laws because they are outward signs of his theology, which flowed from Scripture. Then we turn to Luther's voice itself. Luther's writing holds provocative patterns for language and images for God and humans that are not exclusively male identified. That is, Luther's writing holds cues to help us adopt language for God that is inclusive of female-identified, neutral, queer, and nonhuman images. Lutheran theology helps us past the restrictions of the one-sex and two-sex worldviews and how those worldviews affect language for God.

Luther's Father-Son World

Not surprisingly, as a man of late medieval and early modern Europe, Luther thought the world was properly patriarchal and paternalistic. Men not only made decisions but also ruled in a fatherly fashion. Luther thought human fathers were at the top of earthly relationships and structures, whether in the family and household, the government, or the church. In the 1500s in Europe, these institutions were patriarchal, meaning they were dominated by, identified with, and centered upon men. Men were in charge.

From Luther's point of view, earthly institutions should be administered paternally. That is, the men who ruled should act in a fatherly fashion, no matter their roles. Princes, bishops, emperors, mayors, and teachers, for example, must act in a fatherly fashion. In a sermon on the fourth commandment, Luther writes, "Our prince is our father. Likewise the burgomaster. For God gives us sustenance and guards our homes through the princes as through a father." He also thought that the bishops "who are true Christians" should be honored as fathers.[1]

One way to be fatherly, Luther argued, is to have discipline and obedience in relationships. The central paradigm for relationships is the father-son relationship. Church leaders, parents, teachers, and public leaders should maintain discipline and demand obedience, just as a father expects his children to obey. In lectures on Galatians, Luther wrote,

> For it is legitimate for an apostle, a pastor, or a preacher to reprove those under him sharply in Christian zeal; and such scolding is both fatherly and holy. Thus parents, in fatherly or motherly feeling, will call their son a foolish or worthless fellow, or their daughter a slattern—something they would not stand for if someone else did it. Sometimes a teacher will scold a pupil bitterly, call him a jackass, and beat him with sticks—which the pupil accepts with equanimity, though he would not accept it from a peer or a fellow student. Thus also a magistrate will scold, be angry, and punish.

He continues by saying that the father-son paradigm for relationships makes life go smoothly: "Without severe discipline nothing can be done properly in peace or in war. Therefore unless a magistrate, a clergyman, a public official, or a head of a household is angry and scolds when the situation demands, he is lazy and useless and will never administer his office properly." Although Luther refers to mothers as disciplinarians, the model of being a parent is still fatherly. Fathers should discipline sons harshly, whether they are sons by blood or social contract. Luther is saying that fathers expect obedience and do not act like women or children. He sounds a bit like Aristotle, who used one word for men and fathers because they generate other humans and ideas and a different word to refer to women and boys—because they don't generate other humans and ideas. Luther continues, "Therefore denunciation and anger are as necessary in every kind of life as any other virtue is.

Nevertheless, this anger must be moderated and must not proceed from envy; it must proceed only from fatherly concern and Christian zeal. That is, it must not be a childish or womanly show of temper that is out of revenge; its only desire should be to correct the fault, as a father disciplines his son, not to set his own mind at rest with a desire for revenge but to improve the son by such discipline."[2] Mothers are in danger of acting "womanly."[3] Further, the household needs to be run by fatherly men, even when women have some roles in the household administration and care.

In fact, for Luther, the ideal or "proper" social relationships are based on fatherly leadership. People must keep their places in the household, in the government, and in the church.[4] He writes,

> For you are all one in Christ Jesus. These are magnificent and very glorious words. In the world and according to the flesh there is a very great difference and inequality among persons, *and this must be observed very carefully. For if a woman wanted to be a man, if a son wanted to be a father,* if a pupil wanted to be a teacher, if a servant wanted to be a master, if a subject wanted to be a magistrate—*there would be a disturbance and confusion of all social stations and of everything.* In Christ, on the other hand, where there is no Law, there is no distinction among persons at all.[5]

Luther holds tightly to earthly social positions and views them as established by God, in contrast with life in Christ, in which there is no hierarchical order.

Luther's comments appear to agree with ancient Greek mythology, which suggested that women being in positions of authority leads to chaos. "Womanly" discipline is inferior according to late medieval and early modern understandings of sex because women are considered inferior. Instead, everyone should obey "the father," no matter which earthly fatherly role he has. What Luther says clearly connects to a one-sex worldview.

Lastly, fatherly discipline can be acceptably violent. Fatherly discipline can include "severe" verbal and physical punishment. Men who are not "fatherly" in dispensing severe punishment might even be lazy. But where does this leave sons?

Luther was a son. Luther himself had sons. And he wrote often about fathers and sons. For decades, researchers have debated about Luther's relationship with his father. The story of Luther's conflict with his father is rather legendary and shows how Luther placed trust in God above even earthly fathers and the obedience they demanded. Luther's own life shows when to reject the demands of the father and patriarchy.

After facing the threat of death during a storm, Luther left behind his pursuit of becoming a lawyer to serve as a monk. His father was so displeased with this decision that at one point, Luther wrote it "hit me in the heart" ("traf mich ins Herz").[6] For years he reeled from the estrangement he felt from his father.[7] What comfort Luther had in going against his father's will came from his confidence that human authority, even of a father, is not above the authority of Jesus Christ—who Luther felt was calling him to a religious vocation.[8]

Before any duty to his father, Luther's dependence on God came first. When earthly power, even power that seems to be ordained by God, interferes with Christ, Luther thought social status and authority should vanish in the eyes of a Christian. The pope and the bishops, Luther writes, have interfered with Christ, so he was bold to write, "We reject their social position and say boldly with Paul: 'God shows no partiality.'"[9]

In the same way, he thought, wives should reject the authority of a husband who interferes with Christ. The Word of God trumps "her duty towards her husband."[10] In other words, the priority of Christ shifts how Christians act in the world, sometimes going against expectations of behavior based on the headship of fathers or on sex-based expectations.

At the same time, Luther struggled to bring this paradox together. He remained deeply concerned about "confusion" and a possible loss of "respect and order" in the home and in society. Unfortunately, the glory of being equal in Christ meant little for daily life for Luther. He wrote, "In this world God wants the observance of order, respect, and a distinction among social positions."[11] In many ways, he maintained order by reinforcing gender-based hierarchy. To say it differently, Luther lived in a social and religious context in which "father is best" in so many ways. This one-sex worldview influenced Luther's theology too.

Luther's Father-Son Theology

Luther's theology of God the Father mirrored the headship of fathers he valued in everyday life. In fact, he made a connection from God the Father to the fathers of the world—the actual fathers of families, the fathers of households, and the fathers of governance. In the "Large Catechism," Luther explained that earthly fathers act on behalf of God the Father, for they provide "food, house and home, protection and security."[12] Luther's view that fathers mirror God the Father makes sense in the worldview of his time.

In addition, there was no question about the masculine language of faith.[13] Luther's confession of faith is a good example. As one of many attempts to quiet what he saw as false messages about him, Luther wrote a *Confession of the Articles of Faith* in 1528.[14] He based it on the creeds to show that he was not a renegade leader but an evangelical preacher. He was centrally concerned with the work of the Triune God and the relationship of the three persons of the Godhead. To argue against his critics, he began, "First, I wholeheartedly believe the sublime article of the majesty of God, that the Father, Son, and Holy Spirit, three distinct persons, are by nature one true and genuine God, the creator of heaven and earth."[15] His point is that the God confessed in the creeds is triune, is the true God, and creates and preserves heaven and earth. He does this in the same androcentric language that was part of the historic faith, which made sense in his time.

Even the way Luther talked about Jesus Christ as truly human and truly divine shows the ancient and medieval belief that fathers were *the* source for another human. Remember, according to some historians, as far back as Aristotle, the predominant understanding of reproduction was through the male, also understood as the creator of ideas and civilization. In his exposition of John 1–4, Luther explains in the original German that Jesus is "warer, natürlicher Son Marian, in der zeit von ir geborn, von ewigkeit aber vom Vater gezeuget."[16] In English, this passage literally reads that Jesus is the "true, natural son of Mary, born of her in time, but from eternity fathered from the Father."[17] That last phrase in German is important to notice—to be fathered by the Father. Here is a clear example of a one-sex model. In it, a father fathers legitimate children and, most importantly, sons. Again, God as Father made a lot of sense in a one-sex worldview.

Jesus Christ also has earthly male roles. Jesus Christ, Luther confessed, is alone our Lord and God—"daß Jesus Christus allein unser Herr und Gott ist."[18] He depended wholly on God through Christ, and he explained Jesus Christ's rule in his own life by using male-identified worldly roles. In a dedication letter to his father in 1521, Luther wrote who Jesus Christ was to him personally: "Denn er ist, wie man so sagt, mein unmittelbarer Bischof, Abt, Prior, Herr, Vater und Meister. Einen anderen kenne ich nicht mehr."[19] The key words are recognizable in English: "Then he is, as one says, my unmediated bishop, abbot, prior, lord, father, and master. I no longer know any other." Here we detect Luther's compactly androcentric world, for all authority is explained in male-identified roles.

Luther also shows a one-sex worldview in one of his explanations of Christian identity through Christ. In the same commentary on John 1–4, Luther talks about sonship in a way that reflects the power of fathers and sons—and the *necessity* of sons—in a one-sex worldview. In this passage, Luther connects Christian identity with sonship: "Dieser Jhesus Christus, unser Herr, allein bringt dise geburt, gibet die freiheit, recht und macht denen, die an jn gleuben, das sie Gottes Kinder sind, der gibt alleine die Sonschafft."[20] Luther's confession of faith in Jesus Christ in English reads, "This Jesus Christ, our Lord, alone brings this birth, gives the freedom, justice, and strength to those who believe on him, that they are God's children, he alone gives the Sonship." *Sonschafft* is the key word here. It literally means creation, order, relief, cause, management, or energy.[21] When we think about this unusual word literally, only Jesus gives the Son-relief or the order of the Son. The idea relies on the belief that males are *the* progenitor, the only one who creates life and the only one who has legitimate power.

Not only are God and Jesus Christ male identified, but so are Christians. Luther wrote to his father, who regretted Martin becoming a monk instead of being a lawyer, "So hoffe ich, daß er dir *einen* Sohn Genommen hat, damit er anfange seinen vielen anderen Söhnen durch mich zu helfen."[22] It reads in English, "Similarly I hope that he [God] has taken a son from you so that he begins to help his many other sons through me." Martin, the son of his earthly father and an adopted son of God, wants to serve God's other adopted sons. Extending the theme of adoption in the New Testament, Luther at times refers to God as the king and Christians as adopted sons who are meant to be loyal to the king and to provide the king leading chiefs. The image of Christians Luther evokes is of men in a royal hierarchy.[23] The Christian relationship with God is modeled on father-son relations. You might recall songs with this image, such as "Sons of God," which goes, "Sons of God, hear his holy Word, gather round the table of the Lord."

Imagining God as the king of a royal court, Luther described God's nature as full of wrath and mercy.[24] This contrast of wrath and mercy is one of the central ways Luther talks about Scripture and preaching—and the way God works. He referred to it as law and gospel. It is more than a contrast, though. Many aspects of faith and Scripture were, for Luther, a paradox, things that go together but seem to be against one another. Here are two striking examples of the ways Luther imagined God's wrath and mercy in male-identified metaphors.

Luther described God's law as a violent schoolmaster to boys. Originally written in Latin, Luther wrote, "If he commits something that is against his schoolmaster's orders, he is denounced and scolded by him; what is more, he is forced to embrace and kiss his whip. How wonderful the pupil's righteousness is, that he obeys a threatening and harsh schoolmaster and even kisses his whip!"[25] God's law does not need to serve as a violent disciplinarian forever, Luther thought, but only until "the son [is] made fit for accession to his inheritance."[26] In other words, discipline should bring a child into line with expectations. In the sixteenth century in Germany, it was common practice to make children kiss the whip someone had just used to punish them.[27] While Luther's point appears to be that Christians should not resist God's judgment of human evil, the violence he imagines—or perhaps knew firsthand—is horrible. And Luther's image of God's wrath is identified with stereotypical male violence.

Luther also described God's mercy in a male-identified metaphor as an intimate marriage between God the Father and the Christian son:

> But He is not a Father to me unless I respond to Him as a son. . . . All that remains is that I accept it. This happens when I cry out with that sigh and when I respond to His voice with the heart of a son, saying: "Father!" Then Father and son come together, and a marriage is contracted without any ceremony or pomp. . . . There is only the

Father here, promising and calling me His son through Christ. . . . And I for my part accept, reply with a sigh, and say: "Father!" There is no demand here, but only the sigh of the son, who grows confident in the midst of tribulation and says: "Thou dost promise and dost call me 'son' on account of Christ. I accept and call Thee 'Father.'" This is becoming a son completely without works. But these things cannot be understood without the experience.[28]

Luther experienced his relationship with God as a father-son relationship of claim and assent. Particularly striking is the metaphor of marriage. Although the English translation misses the emphasis in the Latin to the marriage as one without a dowry and thus a union without debt, the metaphor of marriage between God as Father and Christian as son is striking. The sighs and declarations of love and acceptance, of unity and intimacy, and of promise and trust are imagined only in a male-identified relationship here for Luther.

Clearly, Luther put himself in the role of a son in his theology. Luther saw himself as the son of his own father and often perceived Christian life through his own experience of being a son. In fact, upon the death of his father, according to church historian Ian Siggins, Luther referred to trusting in God as a son would trust in his father, even while he was grieving his father's death.[29] This androcentric web of relations and patriarchal order is clear in Luther's earthly order. Given the predominance of the worldview in which "father is best" because the father is understood as the source of life, civilization, and authority, it is not surprising that Luther continued to describe God as Father and Christians as sons.

As I will show, however, despite these strong androcentric images and despite the ultimate authority and power of the father in Luther's theology and ideas about life, elements of his biography tell us something far different. Just as interpreters of Luther advocate taking his political and religious context into account to interpret his ideas about Jews, Muslims, and the pope, we can pay attention to Luther's context related to sex and gender. Doing this gives direction to our own lives of faith. Just as a compass indicates which direction to travel, Luther gives cues to knowing God and our human selves beyond the narrow scope of one dominant sex.

Interpreting Luther through Luther

What I have tried to show so far is that Luther belonged to his time. Men were in charge of almost everything, and Luther thought they should act like fatherly fathers in the world. God was a father, and Christians were sons. God and people lived in a top-down reality, which we saw in a one-sex worldview. In Luther's context, both heavenly and earthly fatherhood were imperial, meaning they were on the top of the cosmic heap. Women were way down in this heap.

To a certain extent, women remained a religious problem even in the midst of the Reformation period. The dominant theological ideas about women in the medieval era focused on the secondary nature of woman in creation. Roughly, the logic ran something like this: Because woman was not created fully in the image of God,[30] she is inferior both physically and mentally to man, who was created in the image of God fully. Due to her inferiority, woman is more likely to make deals with the devil, who was believed to seek weaker beings for "his" handiwork. So to protect society from the devil's work, all women needed to be controlled and protected.[31]

Inherited misogynistic theology fed cultural values about women. For example, artwork and texts about witches in Luther's time said a lot about women. The texts portrayed women as "potential sorceresses,"[32] and artwork by Albrecht Dürer and Hans Baldung Grien, for example, present ordinary women having unwieldy sexual power, a characteristic of woman's weakness. She needed to be kept in order.[33] Images and texts reinforced the idea that women were dangerous and that for the sake of stability, men should control women.

Luther's views about people related to sex and gender were evolving amid cultural and religious views of male superiority. He thought women and girls were valuable and capable, even if he continued to think they were under the authority of husbands and fathers. Luther went even further, though. He did not think they were monsters. He thought they were full persons.

I think aspects of Luther's life and theology can help move the Christian tradition toward full human equality. And I think these same aspects of his life and theology can help move the Christian tradition to language and images for God from all genders. To get at this, interpreting Luther through Luther is crucial. His personal life and pastoral teaching, biblical

Figure 4.1. *Witch Riding Backwards on a Goat*, engraving by Albrecht Dürer, ca. 1500. National Gallery of Art, Rosenwald Collection / Open Access Public domain.

interpretation, writing practices, and theology all reveal important clues and practices that point to the ongoing reformation of the church toward inclusive language and images for God.

Personal Life and Pastoral Teaching: Women and Girls Are Valuable and Capable

Three aspects of Luther's personal life and pastoral teaching disrupted the predominant views about women and men in his time and showed that women and girls are valuable and capable. These three areas included marriage and sex life, education, and inheritance laws.

Luther famously argued that people in religious vocations should marry—and that they should enjoy sexual relations because God created humans to enjoy each other in the bonds of marriage. Five hundred years after former clerics and nuns began to marry, we might forget that Luther's ideas were outrageous at the time. Martin Luther and Katharina von Bora's marriage was itself a scandal, as it was a public acknowledgment of sexual intimacy between a former monk and a former nun. Luther did not think God demanded celibacy. He was breaking with the traditions governing the response of male church leaders to females. Serving the church and being married were not mutually exclusive.

Katie and Martin's marriage is part of the lore of the Reformation. But I did not grasp the social and religious risk they took until I walked the road they walked in Wittenberg for their wedding parade. Although the tradition has waned, you might remember hearing parades of cars with beeping horns through the streets after a wedding, announcing a new marriage and escorting newlyweds from church to reception. Maybe you were part of one or more of these events. When Martin and Katie were married, they walked along one of the main streets in Wittenberg, Germany. People would hang out the upper windows along the road and observe from the roadside. Living and business quarters were compact, so there were presumably lots of people around.

What I did not understand until walking that road myself is that not everyone supported the newly wed Luthers. Some may have jeered; others may have sneered. Some may have even thrown something at them because they opposed breaking what seemed an unchangeable, God-given tradition that clerics and nuns simply do not marry. Even some Reformers were worried Martin and Katie's marriage would risk their work to reform the church. Luther's worst critic called him a pervert. Others said marrying a nun was harlotry.[34] Katie and Martin took a risk getting married. Here were a monk and a nun leaving their vocations, getting married, and publicly saying, by means of a public marriage parade, that they would have sex. Saying that male pastors should marry—and doing so himself—Luther made a positive statement about women.

Another way Luther showed that he thought women and girls matter was through education. He famously advanced universal education for girls, and not simply for elite girls. Education, he thought, was necessary for a good society. Always concerned about the common good and the love of neighbor, Luther wanted everyone to have an education so that they could contribute to good communities and good families. Although he continued to consider men in charge of public life, women and girls still needed education to contribute to managing good households and families.[35]

Luther also embodied the conviction that women and girls are valuable and capable by challenging the inheritance laws of his day. Back then, widows could only keep the original sum of their dowries (what their fathers had paid for them to be married) and personal belongings. Women were not allowed to inherit from their husbands. Luther thought this was wrong. To get around the law, Luther wrote a personal will (rather than an official one) and had close friends sign it, naming Katie as the inheritor so she alone would continue to run their estate, which she had already done for years. His death was not to render her suddenly incapable of doing so, he said in so many words.[36]

Personal Life and Pastoral Teaching: Women Are Not Monsters

Three aspects of Luther's pastoral teaching disrupted the predominant views about women and men in his time: his pastoral care and teaching on arranged marriages, domestic violence, and women's reproductive grief.

In Luther's time, women had little control over marriage and reproduction. Parents customarily arranged marriages for their children, often for economic reasons. They may have needed to expand their land, herds, or other businesses they owned; they may have matched bride and groom based on dowries. Luther knew this, but he also knew that parents sometimes made choices that caused their daughters and sons to be miserable. In response, he implored parents not to force their daughters—or sons—into marriages they did not want. Being forced to live in marriage with someone you did not like, he saw, could cause irreparable harm. He did not think God wanted people to be unhappy simply to fulfill customs. Children, including daughters, were full persons who deserved happiness.

Within marriages, Luther continued to care about women as full persons. Contrary to some of the cultural practices of his time, he argued that husbands should not beat their wives but care for them. Luther even advocated on behalf of a woman under the fist of an exceptionally violent husband and sought legal protection on her behalf while arguing that the husband be held accountable. Yet again, Luther maintained and disrupted standing tradition that is based on a one-sex worldview. Women, he thought, were under the authority first of parents and then of husbands, but he also thought this authority should not be a pretense for hurting or abusing them.

The belief that women are not monsters is most vivid in Luther's pastoral concern for childbearing women. It was not unusual to blame women for not becoming pregnant and for causing miscarriages and stillbirths. He was ashamed of what some pastors told women. Women, he was confident, did not cause reproductive difficulties willingly or on their own. He knew they suffered and wanted only to relieve their suffering. They were not to blame and needed to be cared for as full persons.

Like so much of what we notice when we study Luther, what he said and what he did is mixed. He does not make a perfect path from the old to the new. Yet Luther shifted and challenged what was accepted belief and practice based on sex and gender. He started to offer a renewed understanding of who humans are when we belong to God. And as a formidable student of Scripture, Luther made some remarkable moves in biblical interpretation that also disrupted a male-identified and male-ruled world.

Biblical Interpretation: Eve Is Equal to Adam and an Example for People of Faith

Christians have a long tradition of trying to figure out who we are by reading the first few chapters of Genesis. Some contemporary Christian denominations continue this tradition, but many of them land in the same place as previous generations have. They conclude that women are subordinate to men and not equal in this life. This conclusion reflects both one-sex and two-sex worldviews.

Luther argued that women are not monsters in his interpretation of Eve, and he furthered the ideas that women and girls are valuable and capable in his interpretation of Mary, the mother of Jesus. For Luther, Eve is equal to Adam in sin, redemption, and vocation and an example for people of faith. Eve, Luther argues, is neither the originator of sin nor the shame of the tradition. For Luther, Mary is a partner with God, a true leader, and an example for powerful men. Unlike some Christian interpretations of Mary, she is not simply a demurring, gentle girl in the background of Jesus's life.

Feminist, queer, and other theologians have joined the conversation over what the early chapters of Genesis mean for what is called theological anthropology—theology about humans in relation to God. Two of these feminist theologians, Kirsi Stjerna and Else Marie Wiberg Pedersen, point out that Luther's interpretation of Genesis 1 and 2 begins the important but long-haul work to reorient the Christian tradition's views of humanity away from Greek worldviews. Remember Aristotle's ideas on males and females in chapter 2? Aristotle, who thought women were imperfect versions of men, was one of Luther's pointed intellectual and spiritual nemeses in reforming Christianity. Although Luther repeated some patriarchal views of people, he turns to Scripture to assert that "male and female" in Genesis 1:27 connects to the image of God.[37]

What Luther found, due to his authentic curiosity with texts and his wonder as part of God's creation, Stjerna and Pedersen argue, is that women are truly made in God's own image and not anything but God's very own creation, fully loved and exquisitely made. Luther's biblical conclusions about people matter for language for God. Since Luther revered God as Creator of all, he realized that he could not question God's creation of woman. He revered Eve as the mother of all humanity. Failing to recognize God's power in creating and sustaining woman would be to deny God God's power. Instead, humans should rejoice in the full humanity of woman, who shares equally in God's command for men and women together to have dominion over the rest of creation.[38]

The paradox, Luther thought, is that even though God creates humanity with no hierarchy, due to the fall and God's resulting punishment, woman was inferior to man on earth.[39] In a sense, Luther is like contemporary complementarians who think that humans are equal in value and glory but are made differently for different things—and that females are inferior to males in power and authority.

But there is even more to the story when we read those opening chapters of Genesis in conversation with Luther. Another feminist Lutheran theologian, Kristen E. Kvam, provides fresh insight.[40] Luther's telling of the fall in the garden of Eden, she explains, reorients the predominant habit in the Christian tradition to portray Eve as more evil than Adam and as particularly treacherous. In Kvam's view, Luther shifts Christian understandings of humanity by stressing the equality of Eve and Adam and by interpreting Eve as an exemplar of faith. This was not the usual way to read Genesis.

Primarily, Kvam notes, Luther pointed out that both Eve and Adam disobey God, not simply Eve. And God denounces the serpent but does not denounce Eve and Adam. And Luther, Kvam tells us, noticed God's responses to Adam and Eve when God returns to the garden to confront them. They both are guilty, and they both respond to God in human fashion, with denial and excuses. One is not less fully human than the other.

When God asks Adam if he ate from the tree, Luther wrote, "Here Adam is presented as a typical instance of all sinners and of such as despair because of their sin. They cannot do otherwise than accuse God and excuse themselves."[41] When God asks Eve if she ate from the tree, Luther similarly said, "After unbelief follows the disobedience of all [human] powers and parts. After this disobedience follows later on the excuse and defense of sin; and after the defense of sin, the accusation and condemnation of God."[42] For Luther, Eve and Adam share the human problem of sin.

Not only did Luther interpret Eve and Adam as equal in sin, Kvam continues, but according to Luther, they also equally receive God's mercy and forgiveness while still in the garden of Eden. When God asks them if they ate from the tree, Kvam points out, Luther said they are in the chaos of fear. They do not know what will happen. But once God speaks mercy to them, they are relieved of their fear. Luther wrote, "Wholeheartedly they grasped the hope of their restoration; and full of faith, they saw that God cared about their salvation."[43] Even before they leave Eden, they know they are redeemed.

In addition to their equality in sin and redemption, Kvam demonstrates that for Luther, Eve and Adam also share equally in the human vocation to stand against evil, to fight sin in all the ways it shows up in life. The courage and hope to work against sin come only from God's promise of grace, which is what transforms both of them.[44] Luther emphasized that they are truly and equally God's children in creation, redemption, and sanctification, the ongoing work of the Holy Spirit to mend them and orient them toward the vocation to love God's whole creation.

Perhaps most remarkably, Kvam continues, Luther highlighted Eve's faith as an example for all God's people. Although Luther pointed out that Eve does not perfectly understand what God means when God promises salvation through her descendants, Luther highlighted her unwavering faith, her full-hearted and transparent trust. Eve's faith is so notable that Luther was astonished Eve is not a saint: "Since the pope's church has invented such a vast swarm of saints, it is indeed amazing that it did not give a place in the list to Eve, who was full of faith, love, and endless crosses."[45] Against the grain of the tradition's picture of Eve as the number one sinner not made fully in God's image and the unequal partner to Adam, Luther interpreted biblical texts differently. Luther orients the tradition to understand that people have equal stature, no matter their sex and gender.

Sometimes it also takes reading Luther in his original languages to grasp how Luther's work is even a helpful corrective to some twentieth-century work. Reading carefully clarifies the subtle yet significant messages of some of his biblical interpretation. At times Luther interpreted the Scriptures with distinctive sensitivity to experiences of women and girls and showed that their stories matter for all people of faith.

Biblical Interpretation: Mary Is a Full Person and Leader for God's Work in the World

Most North Americans read Luther's writings in English. There are, after all, well over fifty volumes of his sermons, lectures, letters, and other writings in English; many people worked hard for years to translate from Latin and German into English to produce *Luther's Works*. It has been a standard in scholarship and pastoral education for English readers. But translators sometimes made decisions that make it impossible to pay close attention to some details that matter. How Luther talked about Mary is one of those details.[46]

Mary is an example of a leader, someone Luther thought Prince John Frederick should emulate. Astonishingly, in a world largely ruled by men, Luther told a prince to pay attention to a woman of the Bible. How often in your life have you heard sermons or Bible studies where a woman of the Bible is the model for men—or the whole community? Conversely, how often are men of the Bible the model for women—or for the whole community?

With remarkable insight into Mary's perspective, Luther interpreted the Magnificat, a familiar liturgical song of praise (Luke 1:46–55). For Luther, Mary is a partner with God and a full person with integrity. Luther's voice is so important here. First, it is important to know what the English version looks like because the translators unfortunately make Luther's nuance invisible.

In his explanation of verse 46, the English translation reads, "She lets God have His will with her and draws from it all only a good comfort, joy, and trust in God."[47] In medieval England, the phrase "have his will with her" meant rape.[48] More recently, the phrase "let him have his way with her" is a way to say "he raped her." In an age of increased awareness of sexual violence, this phrase has lost its popularity, but it is important to wrestle with it. Although the translator of Luther's interpretation of the Magnificat may not have intended to imply rape, the image remains in the English text. The problem is that it places the blame for rape on women. Talking about God this way is horrifying. I think there are better ways to talk about God's relationship with us. One of these ways is in Luther's German text.

Luther wrote, "[Sie] läßt Gott in sich wirten nach seinem Willen, nimmt nicht mehr davon denn einen guten Trost, Freude un Zuversicht in Gott."[49] Literally, this reads, "[She] allows God in herself to be host according to/ following his will, taking nothing more from God than a good consolation, joy, and trust." Two details stand out. Mary is a partner with God, and she is a full person through whom God works.

Unlike the English translation, Luther's own words do not make Mary passive because she makes a decision. Mary gives control to God, a loving host. She responds with agency. Also, Mary's personhood is protected; she has her integrity as her own person still, unlike the English version that uses an idiom of unprotected personhood and a loss of integrity. Mary is the full person through whom God works. Unless we read Luther's original German text, we miss these important elements of Mary's full personhood and God's loving relationship with her.

Finally, Mary is a true leader because she trusts and praises God for God's sake, not in order to gain something for herself. According to Luther, there are important differences between God and humans, and he thought that faith, a relationship of pure trust, characterized the way humans need to relate to God. Mary is an exemplar of faith, the kind of faith Luther encourages Prince John Frederick to have, because she trusts God in true humility (allowing God to be her host) and allows the Holy Spirit to work through her.

A Christian's relationship with God comes only through experience in the Holy Spirit, Luther was certain. We simply cannot understand God without the Holy Spirit. He wrote, "Denn es kann niemand Gott noch Gottes Wort recht verstehen, unmittelbar,"[50] which translates to "For no one can rightly or suitably understand either God or God's Word, unless he has [it] unhindered from the Holy Spirit." Said another way, we are not in charge of knowing or understanding God. However, Luther explained, Mary learns about God through the Holy Spirit; through Mary's story, we learn that God lifts up the lowly and puts down the mighty.[51]

The problem is that we grasp at being in God's place. From Luther's perspective, we tend to do the opposite of what Mary did; we lift up our own importance. Luther criticized our vain attempts to be important by pointing out that in this respect, we are the opposite of God: "Es ist hier kein Schöpfer unter den Menschen,"[52] or "There is here no creator among people." Mary, on the other hand, is not inflated with herself, he explains later in his commentary on the Magnificat. Our human problem is that we are not satisfied. Mary was, though.

Mary is the opposite of what Luther calls false preachers, people who do good things and tell everyone around them to do good things because they like to admire themselves and others doing good things.[53] They just want to be noticed. False preachers might also be called false believers because Luther describes them as straying from God when things go badly rather than hanging on to their trust in God like Mary does. Mary knows that God's gifts come from God's hand, not hers.[54] Mary relates to God in humility, the knowledge that she is not in God's place.

Most of us, on the other hand, grasp at importance and being noticed; we tend to make ourselves into idols. This, for Luther, is the central problem: forgetting our relationship of trust in God and our difference from God. Through Mary, Luther rebuked and encouraged Prince John Frederick. In a world of overwhelming male authority and power and female imperfection and insufficiency, this is truly remarkable. Luther's understanding of humans was creating a shift. This is yet another factor to support gender-inclusive language for God because Luther was showing the full personhood of women and girls—of all persons.

Luther's Voice: Writing Practices and Theology

We have just looked at two central biblical characters, Eve and Mary, and the ways Luther's interpretations of them shifted Christian interpretations of them as the mother of sin and a passive, sweet mother of God. Instead, Luther understood both women as exemplars of faith and interestingly disrupted some assumptions about women in a one-sex worldview: women were neither more sinful than men nor incomplete persons. Luther came to these conclusions by studying Scripture carefully and retelling the story. Through Christian teaching, Luther is challenging Christian teaching on sex and gender. His biblical interpretation underscores the fact that views on sex and gender change over time. Taking into account historical changes and Luther's reforms frees us to do the same—to see changes about how to understand sex and gender as positive and to go back again and again to the Scriptures for insight into ourselves and into language and images for God. We, too, retell the biblical stories.

There is yet another element from Luther to support language for God that includes all sexes and genders. He appears to have made choices about certain words in his writings, and from my perspective, his choices have profound effects. Luther often used language for God and humans that was either gender neutral or gender inclusive. The problem is that the power of his words, the power of his voice, is sometimes lost in translation.

Translators must make decisions about words because how you say something in one language is not necessarily literally the same in another language. They must know both languages intimately in order to give the same meaning as the original language. It's not just a matter of knowing the vocabulary because translators are in a sense crossing a communication border; they have to know both audiences and how each uses language. Their decisions influence what people read in the translated language across time and cultures. In some translations of *Luther's Works*, the translators did not use literal translations of phrases and words that matter profoundly.

Some of Luther's original German texts, for example, hold details that are important cues in orienting Christian language for God. Translators of *Luther's Works* often used androcentric words when Luther's original text does not. For example, they changed Luther's references from "children of

God" to "sons of God," from "child of God" to "son of God," and from "God" to "Father." I provide several examples below. Accurate translation matters.

Luther Retains and Transforms Androcentric Language

Luther's writing shows a paradox when it comes to androcentric language. His commentary on John 1–4, written from 1537 to 1540, is one example. Luther gave two important cues to reform androcentric language in Christian faith through how he talks about humans and about God.

Luther talked about human identity in an inclusive way by emphasizing Christ's humanity. Christian identity is not rooted in merits or faults, either collectively or individually. Instead, Christian identity is only through Jesus Christ, a true *human*:

> Komen wir alleine durch die geburt von oder aus Gott, also, das wir gleuben an den namen des Menschen, der Jhesus Christus heisset, warer, natürlicher Son Marian, in der zeit von ir geboren, von ewigkeit aber vom Vater gezeuget.[55]

> We come alone through the birth from or out of God—that is, that we believe on the name of the person, who is called/named Jesus Christ, the true, natural son of Mary, born of her in time, from eternity but fathered from the Father.

As confessed in the Christian tradition, Luther emphasized Jesus Christ as the source of Christian identity—Christian identity is through new birth in Christ, who is fully human and fully divine. Luther emphasized Jesus Christ's humanity (born naturally from a woman) and divinity (literally "fathered" by the Father). Notice that Luther did not emphasize Jesus as the "Son" but as the redeeming human-divine *person* ("Mensch"), whom humans need. At the same time, you might also notice that God as the "fathering" Father fits a worldview of fathers creating legitimate children, especially sons.

But Luther veered away from calling Christians "sons" here. Christians become God's *children* through Christ: "das wir Gottes Kinder warden."[56] And then Luther took another step when he included daughters. Said from

God's viewpoint, Luther wrote, "Ich wil dein Vater sein, und du solt mein Son oder Tocheter sein,"[57] or "I want to be your Father, and you should be my son or daughter." Luther changed the theological scope with language. He showed that humanity is not only about fathers and sons and that Christians are not only sons. Given everything we know about social and religious life that was so deeply influenced by a one-sex worldview, Luther's choices are remarkable.

Children of God, Luther wrote, share equality: "Ich bin so gut als du, ob du gleich Vater, Fürst, Herr, Fraw [sic] bist, denn ich bin eben so wol Gottes Creatur als du,"[58] or "I am as good as you, whether you are father, prince, lord, or lady; then I am equally truly God's creature as you are." Human life in relationship with God means we live in relationship with one another in equality. We might even say that from Luther's perspective, we humans live in relationship with one another in equity.

Unfortunately, Luther again tempered this equitable view of humans. Right after he declared human equality before God, he reinforced a strict order. First, he beautifully echoed the theology that Christians are equally God's children: "Und wenn du ein rechter Christ und Gottes kind bist,"[59] or "And if you are a true Christian and God's child." But then Luther oriented this equality to serve what he called God's order, to which Christians need to be obedient: "So mus auch in der welt der unterscheid der Personen bleiben,"[60] or "So must also in the world the difference among persons remain." Notice that even while Luther used some gender-inclusive language and claimed equality as God's creatures, his cosmic order fits that of a one-sex model. It is like Luther's theology was at odds with the worldview he was living in. His newly reformed and forming theology does not quite get full expression here. However, even while he was embedded in the androcentric language of the Christian tradition, he nudged reformation with the wonderful language of *children* of God and a theology of equality as God's creatures and in identity through Christ.

Luther Disrupts Masculine Language

We return now to Luther's commentary on the Magnificat because it is also a resource to notice Luther's voice through his choices of words. Again, reading from a feminist perspective with empathy and alertness leads to some surprises.

In the English versions of Luther's commentary on the Magnificat, God is predominantly referred to as "Father" or with male-identified pronouns. Humans individually and collectively are also referred to in English with male-identified pronouns and nouns. Luther did not refer to humans as "man," "men," or "mankind." Given his historical context, this fact is compelling. Here are just a few powerful examples of some of the details in his original German.

Even though Luther's predominant view of God is masculine, the translators fortify it. For example, the translators chose to refer to God in the third-person singular pronoun "He," even when Luther wrote "God." In his explanation of verse 48, Luther wrote "so groß angesehen wäre vor Gott,"[61] which is a simple reference to God as God, but the English reads "so highly esteemed by Him."[62] Later in that section, the translators do the same thing. The English reads "and far beneath Him,"[63] but the German reads "und weit unter Gott stellen."[64] Given not only his context but also the language of much of Scripture, Luther *could have* referred to God in these passages as "He" or as "Father." But he did not. Again, he made small decisions with powerful importance. The same is true when we look at how Luther referred to humans.

To explain Luke 1:48, Luther argued that God's eyes look into the depths of humans but that human eyes look to what they think is famous and fancy. The English reads "men's [eyes],"[65] but in German, Luther used the term *Menschenaugen*,[66] or "people's eyes." Shortly thereafter, the English translation is "men," whereas Luther refers to "Leute," or "people."[67] Again, in Luther's exposition of verse 48, the translators used the phrase "totality of mankind," but Luther wrote "der Gesamtheit der Menschen," "the totality of people/humans."[68] These words matter enormously.

The translators' shift to androcentric vocabulary is important because these words are not used exclusively for males in the German language, known for its precision. *Leute* specifically refers to "people" or "folk"; the word should evoke the sense of a mass of ordinary people. *Mensch* refers to "person"; the context can indicate references to a man or a woman, but it most typically refers simply to *a person*. The same is true for the plural. Lastly, the German word *man*[69] means "one," but the translators also used androcentric words for it.

Even more provocatively, the translators moved from "child" to "son."
One full passage helps demonstrate this, first in the translators' English,
then in German, and then in my translation:

> A *son* serves his father willingly and without reward, as his heir, solely
> for the father's sake. But a *son* who served his father merely for the sake
> of the inheritance would indeed be a wicked *child* and deserve to be
> cast off by his father.[70]

> Wie ein *Kind* dem Vater dienet willig umsonst als ein Erbe, nur um
> seines Vaters willen. Und wo ein *Kind* dem Vater nur ums Erbe und
> Gut dient, das ist billing ein feindseliges *Kind* und würdig, daß es der
> Vater verstoße.[71]

> Like a *child* serves the father willingly, without an inheritance, only
> for his father's sake. And where a *child* serves the father only [for]
> inheritance and goods, this is reasonably to be said a hostile *child*
> and deserves the father's repudiation/to be disowned.

Again, Luther referred to the Christian as a "child," not a son. He uses the
masculine pronoun "er" in this passage, a practice hardly surprising given
the priority of sons and boys. Even when he could have easily referred to
Christians as sons though, Luther chose to refer to Christians as *children*
of God. He made a decision with language. And it included more people!
Although a seemingly small move, it is powerful.

A final example of Luther's references to Christians as God's children
helps set up the transition to the next chapter, where we explore more fully
how Luther's theology provides evangelical and theological bases for language for God that is inclusive of all genders. Here is the English version
of a passage in which Luther describes someone who is not a Christian,
one who does not belong to God by faith: "These men are mere parasites
and hirelings; slaves, not sons; aliens, not heirs. They turn themselves into
idols, whom God is to love and praise and for whom He is to do the very
things they ought to do for Him."[72] Yet his German is more expansive:
"Das find eitel Rießlinge und Mietlinge, Diesntknechte und nicht Kinder,

Fremdlinge und nicht Erben; die machen sich selbst zum Abgott und Gott soll sie lieben und loben, eben das ihren tun, das sie ihm tun sollten."[73] Here is a more literal translation: "These are vain pretend/sublords[74] and mercenaries, indentured servants and not children, strangers and not heirs; they make themselves into an idol, and God should love and praise them [and] even/actually do for them what they should do for him." Once again, the English in *Luther's Works* refers to Christians as sons, but Luther refers to Christians as children. Given that the passage refers to heirs, which were generally by law all males at that time, Luther could have easily chosen to refer to Christians as male-identified heirs. Of course, many of the other roles Luther named are male identified. In Luther's world, mercenaries would most likely have been men. Most but not all rulers would have been men. But he still talks about children, not sons.

In this same passage about mercenaries and lords, Luther answered theologically who truly belongs to God. It is not someone who is willing to follow a powerful person's orders, kill for pay, or engage in someone else's war for wages. We might interpret these actions as things that keep some people "low." Luther created a contrast by saying true Christians are children and heirs. The point is that the people who are not true children and (therefore) heirs are people who posture—people who pretend to belong to God, but they do this by making idols of themselves.

If we think about it, this is exactly what a one-sex worldview communicates—that males are best, an idol symbolized in the father-son pair throughout much of history. Luther subtly begins to disrupt the idol through his choice of words and through his theology. From my feminist theological perspective, this is one unexpected but encouraging answer. Luther's choice of words begins to fracture Christian androcentrism.

Luther gives us a fascinating perspective—a point on a Reformation or Lutheran compass. Luther lived in a time when doctors, philosophers, and theologians were still working with the idea that humans shared one sex and that fathers were best and sons were necessary. Yet Luther starts to break open this worldview through his personal life and pastoral teaching, biblical interpretation, writing practices, and theology. Taken all together, these moves could be plenty to make arguments in favor of language and images for God that include all human genders and sexes. In Luther's world, ideas about sex support God as the Father, originator of legitimate heirs, founder of civilization and order, and source of life.[75] As our world continues to move out of a two-sex worldview, we are still struggling with the ways father-son ideals have shaped the Christian church and Christian faith. We have lived long with symbols of fatherhood as well as taken deeply into our hearts and minds the headship of fathers. We, the church, have lived this way for a very long time. I suggest that by now turning to Luther's theology, we will find true north for gender-inclusive language and images for God.

5   Patriarchy and (the) Tradition

A Reformation Compass

It appears that the further from one's own likeness God is, the greater the religious difficulties, even for the faithful.

—Gracia Grindal, "Reflections on God 'the Father'"

Downtown Chicago in December is magical. The air feels thinner than usual, sometimes brutally cold. Pedestrians swarm sidewalks and escalators, streetcars and streets. Music fills the streets, from raucous drums to mellow brass carols. Crowds huddle at windows. Along the famed Michigan Avenue, trees sparkle with stillness, even as taxis honk and rush underneath them. While I know capitalism tries to inhabit Advent and Christmas, for me, that urban convergence of music, lights, and humans is a sliver of holiness. One year someone broke into the pulse of energy and joy. Across the street from the iconic Chicago Water Tower, a white man held a black banner with yellow Bible verses on it and shouted into a megaphone about belief and hell. Faith and fear seemed linked in his message. Just as his presence created discord in the pulsing rhythm of the December city streets, I was struck by how different our views of Scripture and faith were.

When have you realized your understanding of Scripture and faith is different from someone else's? Maybe it happens often for you, or maybe not so often, but Christians have been arguing about how to interpret Scripture and to define faith for hundreds of years. Martin Luther was not the first Christian to have a big, public argument about the Bible and faith. Yet Luther's approach to Scripture began a long legacy of Lutheran biblical interpretation, and his impassioned and biblically rooted view of faith continues to be relevant for Christianity. For Luther, the Scriptures should be read and understood through God's grace in Jesus Christ. And Luther viewed faith as trust, not as having the correct beliefs. These views matter for inclusive language and images for God.

We need a new theological vantage point, a new way forward, because for a long time, Christian theology has embraced predominantly masculine and neutral language and images for God. As I outlined in previous chapters, this is a theological problem. Understanding and worshipping the God of Jesus Christ and even Jesus "himself" exclusively as Father and Son and in andro-centric terms limit Christian faith and life. I think reading Luther through his own theology is an enormous aid in developing other ways to think about Christian faith related to language for God. From my perspective, Lutheran understandings of Scripture and of faith are crucial for embracing inclusive language for God as scripturally, theologically, and evangelically necessary.

Scripture, Faith, and Idolatry

Like the man holding the banner in Downtown Chicago and like people in our own lives, Christians have different views of the Bible and faith. Luther's ideas during the Reformation give us helpful insights for current conversations about the Bible, faith, and even idolatry.

Scripture for Luther was living. It almost reminds me of the Harry Potter characters who talk to someone by writing in a book. They asked questions but got different answers at different times—and the answers were not always entirely straightforward. In a way, Luther thought Scripture was like that. He said that it sometimes communicates God's law, God's condemnation of what we do wrong, while at other times, the very same passage could feel like the gospel, the sweetest proclamation of God's grace.

Luther knew Scripture as living because he experienced God's judgment and God's mercy through it. It was not a rule book to follow literally, as if all things, including words that addressed people in the Bible, could be applied directly to the present. Not every detail or edict was applied equally. Some things, he said, applied only if you were Moses!

But here is the important point with Lutheran biblical interpretation. Scripture points to Christ. This means that the Word as Scripture holds the

Word incarnate, Jesus Christ. Luther described Scripture as a cradle because it tenderly holds Christ for us.[1] There is yet another way Lutherans refer to the Word of God, as gospel. Scripture proclaims the Word as gospel—the good news that God redeems us from our estrangement with God by grace through faith in Jesus Christ, the Word made human. The meanings of the Word of God, you see, are interconnected—as Scripture, gospel, and Jesus Christ. They are each the Word of God (not the words of God) because they are the promise of God's love.

Luther thought everything in Scripture should be interpreted through Jesus Christ. All the weird, confusing, and ambiguous verses, even the controversial ones, should be interpreted through the promise Christians have through Jesus Christ. For example, Lutherans in many parts of the world do not consider a husband to be the head of a wife in marriage and do not follow the practice of head covering for women in worship. The scriptural passages that promote these practices have been interpreted through the gospel of Jesus Christ; the conclusion is that those practices are not considered part of the gospel's message. The practices are not central to God's grace. Yet the image of Jesus Christ as a chicken (and not a Roman rooster) and the twin stories of a shepherd and a lost sheep and a woman householder and a lost coin in Luke *do* make sense when interpreted through the gospel of Jesus Christ because in different ways, they each proclaim God's heartfelt love for us. This is gospel.

Interpreting Scripture through God's promise of grace is freeing. We can read past the injunction for women to cover their heads in worship, for example. We can read more fully the stories and letters and visions in Scripture that deepen faith in Jesus Christ. And faith, for Luther, is a relationship. It is *trust*.

Luther thought humans to be heart creatures, that we live not only because we have hearts that keep us alive by pumping blood but also because we live through our hearts. To live according to our hearts, Luther concluded, shows whom—or what—we trust. Although we might not usually think about idolatry related to our hearts, Luther explained the first commandment this way: "'You are to have no other gods.' . . . To have a god is nothing else than to trust and believe in that one with your whole heart."[2] Luther relies on Romans 10:10 to say the heart is the seat of faith and faith is a relationship of trust. In other words, faith is less about belief (believing certain things correctly) and more about relationship—a trusting relationship with God.

Sometimes we run into problems with this line of thinking about faith, though. We start to act like faith is doing what Jesus did. For Luther, faith is not about doing the right thing; it is about trusting the right God: "For if faith is to be sure and firm, it must take hold of nothing but Christ alone; and in the agony and terror of conscience it has nothing else to lean on than this pearl of great value."[3] Faith is not primarily a guidebook for how to act. Instead, faith begins in trust.

Faith is also not anything we create. "Instead," for Luther, "faith is God's work in us, that changes us and gives new birth from God (John 1:13). It kills the Old Adam and makes us completely different people. It changes our hearts, our spirits, our thoughts and all our powers. It brings the Holy Spirit with it."[4] Faith is different from reason. All the powers God gives us, including reason, are good gifts. The problem with reason, from Luther's perspective, is when we use it on God. We humans are simply not in charge of God. We can use reason to understand faith but not to explain God fully. Instead, we are changed by this lively relationship of trust that faith is. Luther continues in his explanation of Romans:

> Faith is a living, bold trust in God's grace, so certain of God's favor that it would risk death a thousand times trusting in it. Such confidence and knowledge of God's grace makes you happy, joyful and bold in your relationship to God and all creatures. The Holy Spirit makes this happen through faith. Because of it, you freely, willingly and joyfully do good to everyone, serve everyone, suffer all kinds of things, love and praise the God who has shown you such grace. Thus, it is just as impossible to separate faith and works as it is to separate heat and light from fire![5]

Faith changes us. And faith is through the heart.

When the heart is the seat of faith, we risk that something other than God may dwell in our hearts. When that happens, we have an idol for our god. Luther writes, "But in the struggle, when the devil tries to mar the image of Christ and to snatch the Word from our hearts, we discover that we do not know [the words of grace] as well as we should."[6] Some contemporary Christians may not ordinarily talk about the devil working in us, but the point is, forces contrary to the true God can take hold of our hearts.

Perhaps when you think of idolatry, golden calves populate your imagination. You might think of the ways the Israelites were distracted by the golden calf in the wilderness. They defaulted to putting their trust in a statue. When the Israelites were desperate for food, they cried out to God, complaining that God had led them into the wilderness just to die there. When God responded by providing manna and quail, the people hoarded or ate too much. Their actions displayed a lack of trust in God. What was intended as a gift became itself a kind of idol. They trusted the food more than they trusted the one who provided it. This is a reminder of how easy it is to idolize, or trust in, the everyday things in our lives.

Idolatry does strange things to us. Luther puts it this way: "Idolatry does not consist merely of erecting an image and praying to it, but it is primarily a matter of the heart, which fixes its gaze upon other things and seeks help and consolation from creatures, saints, or devils."[7] Idolatry is trusting anything or anyone that is not the true God. Idolatry can include trusting things such as education, capitalism, white supremacy, or patriarchy for our well-being more than we trust God.

When so much was at stake, one of Luther's callings was to make sure people could receive the good news of God's grace. Because he was passionate about making sure people could receive the proclamation of the gospel, he did all kinds of things to ensure it. Luther evangelized. Think about *Luther's Small Catechism*. This compact guide captured the essence of faith and theology in bite-size helpings that people could take in quickly and understand easily. Or think about the dozens of hymns he wrote. They proclaimed the gospel in song.

In North America at least, some Christians define evangelism as knocking on doors and asking if people accept Jesus as their savior. It seems this version of evangelism is often tied to literalist language for God. But I contend that some of Luther's thoughts on being evangelical free Christian language for God from androcentrism. When so much is at stake—when *everything* is at stake—language matters. Language is evangelical because it is one way that Christians proclaim the gospel, and if, like Luther, we think what we say can reach and affect people, we will consider inclusive language as evangelically necessary.

To say it another way, Luther's grasp of humans as creatures in a relationship of trust with God means we need relational language that disrupts possible idolatry—that is, trust in something other than the true God. I think we Christians sometimes put misplaced trust in androcentric language. We treat it as if it is God.[8] But we have an opportunity through Lutheran theology to embrace feminine, female-identified, queer, nonbinary, masculine, and male-identified language for God. Key elements of the evangelical Reformation movement matter for language for God. To say it again, Luther helps us realize that for language to be evangelical, it needs to be able to affect the heart, to transform hearts to trust and honor God. What does it take to affect hearts? A glimpse into the field of psycholinguistics gives some insight into how language works more generally before we turn to what Luther says about language.

Language Affects Human Spirits

The ELCA teaches in its social statement *Faith, Sexism, and Justice: A Call to Action* that this church believes that God does not desire patriarchy.[9] Relying on what language experts say, the social statement also says language about humans or about God can work for or against a male-favored, masculine-centered world. I think that exclusively masculine language for God (or for humans, for that matter) is idolatrous because it leads us to misplaced faith—faith in what is only masculine or male identified. Language is powerful, and it shapes us.

People who study language and psychology know that language is creative and interactive—or, said another way, that humans are creative and interactive with language. I heard one of these researchers on the radio, and she helped me think more deeply about the evangelical nature of language. Jean Berko Gleason has studied linguistic development and its effects on people for decades. In a nutshell, she finds that humans are innately creative with language and that linguistic development is intensely interactive. As children, we learned to mimic what we heard, even when we did not know what the words all meant. Think, for example, of all the songs and rhymes we use with children when they are learning to talk. How adults and children alike learn and interact with and through language, she concludes, shapes our spirits and our communities.[10] Her research points to the flexibility and freedom of language and its value for human life because it speaks to and supports the human spirit's development. We learn to communicate through words. We learn how to create meaning with others.

At the same time, what we learn and internalize through early language development and things we learn later in life are difficult to reconcile with one another.[11] Some of Berko Gleason's earliest research shows that when adults teach children ritualized language, actual words (what is called a linguistic form) come first and meaning comes later. That is, children learn the "proper" *form* of words and only later start to understand their meaning.[12]

Think of hymns and other songs you sang as a child. Like other children, you likely learned the form of the words first; the meanings came later. Sometimes, what is really being said with words becomes clear only much later. For example, think about this fun song from Christian education, of which a friend reminded me:

Father Abraham had many sons.
Many sons had Father Abraham.
I am one of them, and so are you.
So let's just praise the Lord!

The song claims that all Christians are *sons*. As I have said, saying a Christian is a son of God and, in this case, a son of Abraham is full of meaning that children will not necessarily be able to digest. But taking this language into our hearts shapes us. As research makes clear, because language is encoded, we are shaped by its meanings, whether we are conscious of it or not.[13] Only later might we struggle to reconcile our lived experience with the meaning of the words we learned.

Here is another example of androcentric language, but this example shows how people change language when our understanding changes. In the 1950s, most married women in the United States were referred to by their husbands' first and last names (Mrs. Thomas Peters). It was like saying they were "Mrs. Man." The code embedded in this naming convention is that a married woman was identified with a man and belonged to him; he was her head. Few women in this country use this naming now. As women began to think differently and to refuse male-spouse-identified names for themselves, practices changed. Changes in language reflect changes in our thinking.

Language Is Evangelical

We might say the same about God and language for God. How has male-identified language for the three persons of the Trinity shaped you? How we understand God relates to the language we use, whether that "language" is in titles, metaphors, or images. If we are going to proclaim the gospel of Jesus Christ in order to reach actual people so that their hearts are truly transformed by the power of the Holy Spirit, we need to use evangelical language—language that actually proclaims the gospel of God's grace to real people. We will use language or images that proclaim who God is and what God has done for us. Luther writes, "When a preacher preaches in such a way that the Word is not frustrated in producing fruit but is efficacious in the hearers—that is, when faith, hope, love, patience, etc., follow—then God supplies the Spirit and performs powerful deeds in the hearers."[14] Luther takes us right into realizing the power of language. For the Word of God to be effective, we need words that do not frustrate the Word of God for people.

Think about the streets of Chicago in December again. The street preacher did not evangelize me effectively. The Word was frustrated. In this relationship of trust with God, I think we are responsible for paying attention to the words and images we use. Not just women are attuned to this issue of language as well. After being away from church services one summer, my husband was overwhelmed with the masculine language of the liturgy. "Had I become so used to that masculine world that I could no longer notice it?!" he wondered aloud. He did not know how to worship again. People who are queer feel the lack too, like Magdalena in chapter 1, who felt known when she saw a painting of Jesus pregnant, or like pastors I know who identify as nonbinary and hunger for gender-neutral language and images for God. As Lutheran theologian Gracia Grindal said long before some of the most vigorous public theological debates about language for God, "It appears that the further from one's own likeness God is, the greater the religious difficulties, even for the faithful."[15] What language is necessary for faith?

The ways Luther linked evangelism and the language of faith simply take away any requirement that Christians use only masculine language to proclaim the gospel or to understand the Trinity. Luther's own conviction that language is a matter of the heart in faith helps us resist the bondage of a gender and sex binary and hierarchy in the language of faith. Instead, I think Luther's theology helps us live with paradoxical language for God. That is, I think Luther's theology helps us embrace language for God that includes every and all genders.

The next step is to look at what he says about language. In my study of Luther, I have found that for him, the language of faith needs to be relational, gospel bestowing, digestible, and imagistic. From my perspective, Luther's theology of the Word frees Christian faith from exclusively masculine pronouns for God and even an exclusive male identity for our understanding of Jesus Christ.

The Language of Faith Is Relational: Words Bear the Word

The language of faith is relational because Scripture is relational.[16] Paying close attention to what Luther said about Scripture, we can make two distinctions. The character and the content of Scripture are relational.

The character of Scripture is relational because it reaches out to people. In other words, God speaks through all the images evoked through words to claim people.[17] Biblical images, whether parable or psalm, bear God's presence to people. Lutheran theologian Robert Goeser, in explaining how important language and arts are in the Lutheran tradition, says Luther thought language is fully able to bear God's presence because we already know that the Word is God and bears God's presence.[18] All those words in the Bible bear God's presence for us. Scripture is relational because through its words, it reaches people.

The content of Scripture is also relational because, as noted above, it holds Christ, its treasure and center.[19] Another way Luther talked about the Word (as Scripture) is that it "carries" Christ—it carries Christ to all. This means for Luther that God claims people through Christ through the words of Scripture. The content of Scripture is active.

Yet Luther made an important distinction. All of Scripture is surely God's Word, he thought. Some of it is clear, and some of it is hard to understand. The parts that are clear, he thought, are about Christ. For the parts that are hard to understand, the fault is ours; we just don't know enough to make sense of them. Some parts of Scripture are directed at particular people, and other parts are directed at everyone. He warned against getting confused about this difference.

While he respected all of Scripture as God's Word, he chided people not to be distracted by the parts that are not spoken to us. He preached that some people run around saying, "God's word, God's word," as if it all applied to everyone's lives through the ages.[20] For example, you're not Moses? Then don't expect God's command for Moses to strike a rock for water to apply to you. You're not Sarai? Then don't expect God's promise of a son in your elder years to apply to you.[21]

On the other hand, the gospel applies to everyone. We all "belong under the gospel."[22] This—the content of Scripture—does apply to you because it applies to everyone. And the gospel is itself all about relationship, for as Luther pointed out, God's Word that applies to us is that we preach, trust God through Christ and be baptized, and love our neighbors as ourselves.[23]

What could be more relational? The words of Scripture bear the Word for us so that we might love God and neighbor. It's a little bit like poetry, maybe. The words on the page are in one respect a bunch of letters put together to make words. But poetry as words put together bears something to us—beauty, emotions, recognition. Luther is saying something similar about the language of faith by stating that words (together) bear the Word to us so that we might trust God's love.

The Language of Faith Is Gospel Bestowing: Through Words, the Word Affects the Heart

Christ prints the gospel on our hearts. Luther wrote, "This gospel our Lord Christ has produced, brought about, and left behind as a legacy. First he imprinted it upon the apostles' hearts and then, through the apostles' successors he continued to imprint it upon more and more Christian hearts, besides also letting it be preserved visibly in books and pictures."[24] Think about the image of the heart here again. It is as if Luther is saying that the words of Scripture are not making grand, convincing arguments so that we can reason ourselves into faith. Instead, the words of Scripture work in us. They become written in our hearts, much like poetry or songs can become written in our hearts. Said another way, words bring God's love to us not as a well-reasoned argument but as what transforms us *because* they bring the gospel to us. As Luther sees it, Christ works through the images that language produces to build a relationship with us. To affect our hearts, though, the words of the Word need to be digestible.

The Language of Faith Needs to Be Digestible

Maybe because he liked food or maybe because he had digestion problems, Luther liked to talk about digestibility when he discussed Word and sacrament. He knew firsthand how awful it was not to be able to digest food well, and he extended the metaphor to the language of faith. You might recall that Luther taught that Word and sacrament are the means of grace—how God is with us in this earthy, messy life. We do not earn grace through our attempts to be holy. We don't earn it through the things we do—even if they are really great—or the professions we have or the status of our family.

Think about communion, the sacrament of the Eucharist. Lutherans teach that God is in, with, and under the elements of bread and wine. We are able to digest the living Christ, whether as juice or wine, wafer or bread, gluten-free or wheat-filled. It is easy to understand how we need to be able to digest the elements of communion.

It is the same with the words of the Word. We need to be able to take them in. The words need to be digestible for us. The words from the preacher's mouth (or printed sermon) need to come in forms we can digest. The tone, the volume, and the actual words used to reach someone all matter. In thinking specifically about language, if the words are not digestible, other words need to be used. This matters so much because, to say it again, Lutherans believe the Word is one of the means of grace. The Word simply must be digestible, and for Luther, this digestible language of the heart is imagistic language.

The Language of Faith Is Imagistic

During the Reformation, Germany experienced a great deal of havoc. One chaotic situation Luther addressed was the violent toppling and destruction of religious images. Some leaders at the time used their influence to compel the destruction of images or helped create laws against any religious images. The situation upset Luther.

As with other contentious issues during the upheavals of his era, Luther turned to and relied first on God's promise that Christians are redeemed by grace through faith. Images in churches and homes do not threaten faith, he thought, if God's Word is what dwells in hearts. When God resides as the host of our hearts, no image of eye, ear, or mind can be an idol. The problem, he argued, was when people worship the image itself and not God or when people think that creating or simply having an image of God *pleases* God and earns God's favor. So Luther told people that tearing images down is needless and misguided. If you worship an image in your heart, then you have the problem of unfaith.[25] Imagery, Luther knew, could lead to idolatry because imagery affects the heart.

However, Luther also thought images are central to the language of faith because imagery affects the heart, the seat of faith.[26] While Luther did not want Christians to worship images, graven or imagined, he explicitly urged extraordinary, evocative language for faith: "We would act more correctly if we left dialectic and philosophy in their own area and learned to speak in a new language in the realm of faith apart from every sphere."[27] Theological language cannot bear the exactness of philosophical language, of reason. The language of faith enlivens us, not with facts, but through words bearing the Word. Again, we see here how necessary poetry, metaphor, and symbols are.

Words were central to evangelism for Luther, and he wanted them to be beautiful and speak to people about what mattered. Even all the important theological arguments he made against opponents mattered less, in a sense, than imagistic language. Luther shared with one correspondent, "I am persuaded that without knowledge of literature pure theology cannot at all endure. . . . I see that by [poetry and rhetoric], as by no other means, people are wonderfully fitted for the grasping of sacred truth and for handling it skillfully and happily."[28] How vital are the words tumbling and flowing through sermons and hymns, through Sunday school lessons and liturgy!

At the same time, Luther also made sure to translate the Bible using evangelical, imagistic language. For a long time, the Scriptures were read in church services in Latin. But not everyone understood Latin. So Luther spent years translating the Bible from Hebrew, Greek, and Latin into German. It was an enormous project that took many years and gave Luther fans and critics alike.

To state the obvious, German is different from Hebrew, Greek, and Latin. It has different sentence structures and different nuances. And people speaking German in the 1500s were different from the ancient Israelites speaking Hebrew and the early church priests using Latin. Languages and times have different sensibilities and different figures of speech. However, Luther was certain that the Word as Scripture needs to provoke imaginations; through images in Scripture, God works faith in people. Luther gave himself to their power, stating, "I don't know what sort of power images have that they can so forcefully enter and affect one, and make every[one] long to hear and speak in imagery." To make figurative language literal "for the benefit of the uneducated," Luther continued, stripping language to its "crude and simple sense" is a terrible idea because it would no longer be evangelical.[29]

As I wrote in the previous chapter, translators make decisions about how to communicate in one language what is said differently in another. Sometimes, as I pointed out, literal translations are necessary. At other times, they are not. Either way, translations need to bear images that people can digest.

When Luther translated the Psalms, for example, he ran into at least one outspoken critic who did not like the fact that Luther prioritized *the message* of Scripture over the literal translation of it. For example, he chose *not* to translate all second-person pronouns from Hebrew into German literally.

Why? Luther changed things up because he thought the most important thing to do was to make sure Germans knew God's grace in their own language, and a literal translation of the Hebrew was getting in the way of that. Proclaiming the gospel took center stage over literalism. Luther defended dismissing literal translation when it gets in the way of gospel proclamation: "We have made changes of this sort several other times as well. That may perhaps irritate Master Know-it-all, who does not bother about how a German is to understand this text but simply sticks to the words scrupulously and precisely, with the result that no one understands the text. We do not care. We have taken nothing from the meaning."[30] The gospel needs to reach hearts, and hearts need the language of faith and its images.

Luther is a guide here. What he said about faith, hearts, relationships, and the gospel serves as a compass for us to move into language and images for God that are inclusive of all genders. Luther's theological convictions make clear that the language of faith is relational, gospel bestowing, digestible, and imagistic. Because language and images for God that are exclusively or mostly male identified or masculine are not digestible for many people and get in the way of the proclamation of the gospel, language for God cannot be entirely or even primarily male identified. If some words and images are not able to bear the Word to someone, other words and images need to be used. Inclusive language for God is an evangelical necessity.[31]

The origin of evangelical faith (these Reformation ideas) and the basis of evangelical faith (Jesus Christ) orient Christian life together in faith. We head into old but new territory with the help of a Reformation compass. Luther's convictions help Christians embrace language for God that is of no gender and of many different genders. Using many paradoxical images in language for the three persons of the Trinity is responsive to the evangelical and theological reforms Luther urged for the sake of the free course of the gospel—for us.

The Word of God Baffles Gender Literalism

Just as evangelical language needs to be multigendered to proclaim the Word and to evoke faith, the Word of God is not sex or gender specific. We are going to think a little more deeply with Luther about the Word of God because some

Lutheran insights about it in fact baffle what I call gender literalism. First, we consider the meaning of the Word and then the character of the Word.

The Meanings of the Word of God Are More Than Manly

As is already clear, Lutherans and many other Christians refer to Jesus, the Bible, and preaching as the Word of God. One scholar points out that Luther also referred to God's creative and redeeming speech and Christian life itself as God's Word.[32] But how can the Word of God be all these things at the same time?

A number of Christians read the Bible in a literal way, meaning that they think the Bible contains the literal words of God.[33] Read this way, Jesus as Son and God as Father are linked to masculine understandings of God. This can have several consequences, including husbands following Jesus as, for example, "the Original Catholic Alpha"[34] and certifying only males for ordained ministry. Thinking with Luther both complexifies and clarifies what the Word of God is. For Luther, the Word of God is so much more than manliness, manhood, or masculine language.

The Word of God is the life-giving proclamation of God's promise of grace and mercy through faith in Jesus Christ.[35] In the "Large Catechism," Luther wrote about the Word of God as living and lively, as the force that grounds and shapes Christian life: "God's word is the treasure that makes everything holy.... At whatever time God's word is taught, preached, heard, read, or pondered, there the person, the day, and the work is hallowed, not on account of the external work but on account of the word that makes us all saints."[36] The Word is not a static teaching, a set of dogmas, the printed words of the Bible, or Jesus as a heroic example.

Instead, it is living. It is beyond human control. It redeems and shapes Christians. So for Luther, the Word of God is active, creative, redemptive, and original. The Word of God is first and foremost *event*.[37] The Word happens. And the Word "happens" in a variety of ways. Here is a brief explanation of the five I've mentioned—and each of these meanings of the Word of God baffles gender literalism.

The first meaning of the Word of God is *God's speech*. God speaks, and that holy speech creates out of the void and redeems. This is the Word of God. We know all about the ways God creates and redeems through images in the Bible, like the way God creates a way out of no way[38] through the Red Sea for the Israelites fleeing slavery in Egypt or the way God saves by lifting the young on wings like a bird.[39] God acts. What does this mean for us in terms of gender? God speaking and acting the promise of grace is not necessarily male identified.

At the same time, *Jesus Christ* is God incarnate. This is a second meaning of the Word of God. Jesus Christ is the embodied promise of God, the embodied declaration of God's grace for us. Although we know Jesus as a man through the Gospels, the incarnate Word of God does not need to be male identified because the point of the incarnation was that God became human, not that God became a male.[40] Incarnation would mean little to anyone but men if the point of God's presence among creation was to be male. What does this mean for us in terms of gender? Jesus Christ as God incarnate can be unhinged from exclusive maleness and even shown in the arts in ways that baffle gender categories and expectations.

A third meaning of the Word of God is the Word as *Scripture*. Scripture as the Word of God has unfortunately shifted to mean all of the Bible as the literally spoken words of God, all of which should be understood as the rigid last word on Christian life. For Luther and much of the Lutheran tradition, nothing could be further from the truth. Scripture carries Christ. It acts rather like a medium that carries God's spoken Word of creation and redemption to people. Scripture, as written Word, is not a static treasure of literalism, which can mire the Christian tradition in androcentrism, but bears the gospel. We should expect to meet Christ, Luther writes, for engaging Scripture rightly "is nothing else than Christ coming to us, or we being brought to [Christ]."[41] For Luther, the purpose of Scripture is that it is "a means . . . to faith . . . the vehicle of the Holy Spirit."[42] What does this mean for us in terms of gender? What Scripture bears—the gospel, God's promise—is not male identified, and certainly neither is preaching.

Preaching is a fourth meaning for the Word of God. When the preacher preaches, God's Word is present and active in those who hear the message. Through words spoken in particular contexts to people's hearts, the preacher bestows the Word. In other words, contextually specific words bestow the transcendent Word. Preaching is *for* us—in all our particularities and all our similarities. Preachers preach to specific people. What does this mean for us in terms of gender? Preaching as the Word of God is not male identified because preaching is made of the words bearing the Word—words that hover in the air, words that lodge in the heart, words that *are* event. This Word is not male or male identified.

And all the preached words of the Word shape *Christian communities.* This fifth sense of the Word of God, even though not part of ordinary Lutheran teaching, is the church living as the Word of God, bearing the gospel. The church lives not only through preaching and administering the sacraments of baptism and communion but also as the whole people of God as the Word of God, even in its ordinary days. The Word of God is in the actual words the church speaks and in its ordinary and unusual actions—in the church basement, at work, in the street, or wherever. What does this mean for us in terms of gender? To say it again, the Word of God as the life of the church is not male identified because the body of Christ is made of people of many genders and sexes.

Understanding the Word as God's speech, the incarnation, Scripture, preaching, and Christian life makes clear that the Word is not simply Jesus the man or a literal reading of the Bible. The Word is God's lively means of grace. The Word has no exclusively gender-based identity. Simply put, Luther characterizes the Word of God in a gender-inclusive way.

The Character of the Word of God Is Queer

Reading Luther brings to the surface characteristics of the Word that do not depend on a gender-based binary but instead speak of divine characteristics. For Luther, the Word of God is paradoxical, generative, transformative, powerful, and effective. None of these characteristics is exclusively masculine. You could even say the characteristics of the Word of God are queer because it queers a gender or sex binary.

The Word as gospel is *paradoxical* because it is both proclaimed and visible. When the Word is proclaimed, it is said out loud, sometimes even shouted out loud. It is a busy, loud, and noticeable occurrence! God is present and at work in the words of the Word. The Word proclaimed is around us and surrounds us, envelops us.

At the same time, the Word is visible, Luther thought, in the sacraments of baptism and the Eucharist. Baptism involves water, and communion involves bread and wine. But in the sacraments, these ordinary things are not just taken as they appear; *with* the Word, they bear God's promise of forgiveness and new life. The sacraments are paradoxes because Lutherans believe that God is in two places at the same time: in heaven and in the water, bread, and wine.[43] From this perspective, God is in human speech—the Word proclaimed—and in the elements. The Word is God's promise of comfort and grace, incarnate in Jesus Christ and paradoxically proclaimed and visible.

The Word is also paradoxical because it is law and gospel. The Word of God is law because it shows us that we do not save ourselves. The law condemns how we harm others and the ways we cling to idols. The Word of God is gospel because it brings us consolation and frees us from bondage to all the ways we think we can save ourselves. The gospel proclaims God's grace for us.

The Word of God for Luther is *generative* because it gives and sustains life. "For once the pure and certain Word is taken away," Luther was convinced, "there remains no consolation, no salvation, no life."[44] Without the Word of God, everything vanishes. We won't make it. Luther even used an explicitly generative metaphor to talk about the life the Word gives to Christians as heirs of God "born of the Word, which is the divine womb in which we are conceived, carried, born, reared, etc."[45] When Luther worried about the purity of the Word of God, he was not talking about biblical literalism; he was talking about this most central treasure that the Word is God's act to save *us*.

The purity of the Word of God is about stripping us of all the ways we try to convince ourselves that we are doing a nice job of getting God to like us or of getting ourselves back to God.[46] Luther referred to the Word of God as God's womb when he explained Isaiah 46:3: "*Who have been borne by Me from your birth, carried from the womb. . . .* Here consider God's zeal and care for us. Is not the maternal instinct constantly concerned about the infant? So God cares for us with an everlasting maternal heart and feeling. *Womb*. The fetus knows no concern. All the concern is in the mother, who looks after her tender belly. So God is likewise concerned for us." If we are not in the womb of God, we won't survive. We depend on God as our source. Luther continued, "The Lord will reject no one, however weak, if only we cling to the Word, the womb of God. Thus, then, we must believe in our weakness that we are borne in the womb of God, who will care for us with supreme devotion and will never reject us."[47] Being in God's womb, the Word is not only for individuals but also the generative source of the church. The Word as womb gives and sustains life.

As we have seen in some of Luther's other ideas about the Word of God, it changes us. It is *transformative*, and it transforms us by nourishing us. It is the food of Wisdom, Luther pointed out.[48] As Holy Wisdom, God's Word works in us similar to how poetry affects the heart rather than how laws or church teachings curb our behavior. Luther thought that the Word of God massages our hearts, makes us new, transforms us in ways we could not have predicted. This kind of transformation is deep within us because of the way God relates to the seat of our relationships, our hearts. Luther thought the Word not only lives in Christian hearts;[49] the Word imprints hearts.[50] Our hearts change. And when the Word has imprinted hearts and transformed

Figure 5.1. *Hagia Sophia*, painting by Meinrad Craighead, 1987. Reprinted by permission.

them, the Word has made the church holy;[51] the gospel makes Christians holy and free.[52]

Being made holy and free doesn't just happen once and then we move on. Instead, the Word of God, as Luther put it, is *effective* in human life. It creates and sustains faith. Luther wrote, "And just as [God] initially gives us faith through the Word, so later on [God] exercises, increases, strengthens, and perfects [faith] in us by that Word." We cannot match this power to create faith, to redeem, to save from bondage. The Word is simply *powerful* in ways humans are not. So he continued, "The supreme worship of God . . . is . . . to hear and read the Word."[53] Nothing is more central to faith.

Tracing Luther's ideas illustrates the ways the Word of God does not need to be masculine or male identified. None of these characteristics depend exclusively on one side or another of a gender binary. The Word of God baffles gender literalism and a gender binary. I think Luther helps us affirm language for God that includes many different genders, queered language that may be simultaneously feminine and masculine, baffling the extremes of a binary.

Yet one more piece of Luther's theology helps us understand how all genders and no genders matter in language for God. Although ordained pastors in his day were all men, Luther's theological reflections on ministry have little use for gender-based preferences. What I mean is that even though Luther supported men as pastors, his theology of ministry itself relies on no particular gender. Here again we see his deep theological convictions serving the proclamation of the Word yet disrupting even his own notions—the idea that pastors are only males. From my perspective, this is another aspect of Lutheran theology that helps us understand that God is not only masculine.

A Theology of Ministry Baffles Gender

Thinking our way out of an androcentric tradition relies on generous and attentive reading. I see yet another remarkable line of thought in Luther's theology of ministry, and it connects directly to the way I understand Luther's convictions about the Word. Neither Word nor ministry is exclusively male identified. In a famous treatise, *On the Babylonian Captivity of the Church,*

Luther argued with church authorities about ministry and ordination. Outraged that priests were preoccupied with their titles, authority, and garments, Luther tried to bring the focus of ministry back to the Word. "It is the ministry of the Word that makes the priest and the bishop," he argued. "Whoever does not preach the Word . . . is no priest at all."[54] And he pressed his point further when he wrote, "Furthermore, the priesthood is properly nothing but the ministry of the Word—the Word, I say; not the law, but the gospel."[55] In fact, Luther lovingly referred to ministry as bestowing the gospel.

From Luther's perspective, ministry was perpetually Word oriented. "There remains nothing for the office of the ministry or the office of preaching," Luther implored, "other than this single work, namely, to bestow or to present the gospel which Christ commanded to be preached."[56] Ordained pastors bestow the gospel.

Bestowing the gospel, for Luther, depended on God's action through ministers.[57] Gospel proclamation does not depend on who or what someone is. God's command, Luther said, "causes the hand of the priest to be the hand of Christ."[58] In wild opposition to the rules about ministry in his time, Luther argued that the body, mind, or soul of the person bestowing the gospel did not matter. He said they do not need to be celibate, without sin, or high in church status. From this perspective, people of any and all genders, races, and abilities are servants of the Word in preaching, baptism, and communion. Said in a parallel way, ministers do not need to be male, white, and without disability.

Through a theology focused on God's work in us and gospel proclamation, Luther gave an explanation to undercut the theological argument that ministers needed to be modeled after Jesus Christ and therefore needed to be male. To bear the Word does not depend on body parts. If we think about the history of the meaning of bodies, we know that body parts have for so long been used to argue that some people are, in their very beings, inferior to others—that people with dark skin are inferior to people with light skin and that persons with female anatomy are inferior to persons with male anatomy. From a Lutheran perspective, none of these characteristics make someone "worthy" or "correct" to be a minister. Instead, God's Word does. Bearing the Word for the sake of faith of others—which is centered in the heart—does not depend on biology or gender identity.

Luther reoriented a theology of ministry because he was focused on God working in and through humans, not on people being a particular kind of human who deserves to be a minister of the Word. Through Luther's ardent reforming convictions regarding the Word of God, we have a Lutheran perspective that neither the Word of God nor the minister of Word and sacrament must be exclusively male identified or masculine. With the help of the Lutheran theological tradition, we are freed to embrace female-identified and queer language for God because both the Word and ministers of the Word are multigendered. In the last part of this chapter, we turn to the central Lutheran teaching that we are justified by grace through faith because it, too, clarifies the theological necessity of language and images for God of all genders and no gender.

Justification by Grace through Faith Disrupts Male Idolatry

When I think about justification by grace through faith, I think of seams in an article of clothing. We all wear clothes sewn by someone, maybe even by ourselves. Someone brought pieces of fabric together. Each piece of cloth is distinguishable; some pieces are straight and some curved or at a sharp angle. When pieces of fabric are brought together so that the edges align, it is called justifying the seams. For the garment to be beautiful, comfortable, and useful, pieces need to align. Otherwise, our clothes would not fit well. They might chafe our skin or restrict our free movements.

I wonder if when God justifies us by grace through faith, it's more than being "made just" by being exonerated in God's courtroom. I think it is also being made complete. We are woven together into something new. Our edges are aligned, made even with God's edges. We become aligned with God's intention, God's grace, God's love, God's future breaking in right now. And from a Lutheran perspective, we are unable to justify our edges with God or with one another. We are aligned with God not by our own power but through the power of the Holy Spirit, who "calls us through the gospel," as Luther says in his explanation of the third article of the Apostle's Creed in *Luther's Small Catechism*.

I gather that Luther also thought beyond the courtroom scene when he discussed justification because his experience of justification was full of emotion. He knew firsthand that our relationship with God creates joy and freedom. When he created the now well-known Luther rose, he explained to a friend how it symbolized joy: "Such a heart is to be in the midst of a white rose, to symbolize that faith gives joy, comfort, and peace; in a word it places the believer into a white joyful rose."[59] So in contrast to the cold language of the courtroom scene, Luther speaks about the experience of justification with lilting emotion.[60]

In addition to talking about the *experience* of justification, Luther also talked about the *doctrine* of justification. Lutheran theologians describe the doctrine of justification as promise and judgment. It is God's promise to save the entire cosmos, and it is God's judgment against anything that tries to replace God's promise of grace with human-made laws, rules, or ideals. The doctrine is not faith itself. Faith is trusting God's promise of grace, not trusting the doctrine. The doctrine is simply teaching about faith.[61] What I am going to share is critical thinking as a feminist Lutheran about faith in conversation with Luther's ideas.

Luther's experience of God's grace so reoriented his faith that he staked his life on it and called justification by grace through faith the doctrine by which the church stands or falls. It orients everything else there is to say about faith, and it orients how to interpret and translate Scripture.

While Luther's conviction is powerful, I am drawn to the doctrine of justification not simply because he was excited about it but because the center of this doctrine is God's love for us and our dependence on God. In fact, I think the doctrine's dual disruption and affirmation are central to a theology for inclusive and expansive language. In short, the doctrine of justification disrupts idolatry and bondage and affirms the freedom of a Christian.

Because the doctrine of justification is completely centered on God and Jesus Christ, it disrupts idolatry. Remember, Luther thought idolatry was trusting something or someone who is not the true God; it is trusting ideas we create. Idolatry is letting the heart be guided by human values. As we saw in the chapters on the history of sex, in the United States, we have a long history of creating and trusting male supremacy and white supremacy. Faith in God understood through the doctrine of justification disrupts male idolatry and white idolatry. God is not a white man with a flowing beard. God is not a man, so God is not known only by masculine pronouns or through masculine characteristics, stereotypical or otherwise. God is not white.

The doctrine of justification also disrupts bondage. It declares freedom from bondage. Usually in the Lutheran tradition, we talk about freedom from the bondage of sin, death, and the power of the devil. While we might affirm this as certainly true, what does it mean concretely to say we are freed from bondage? I think one form of bondage is the gender-based binary. We saw how it was created in the 1800s in the two-sex worldview. This idea that humans are created in only one of two opposite sexes puts people in bondage, bondage to ideals we have created in order to keep particular people in power with the perverse idea that they are better than the rest of humanity. This bondage kills people by forcing them to try to adhere to the rules we've made up about what it means to be masculine or feminine. Many Christian denominations even have teachings about the binary that I would call gender-based righteousness—that we'll please God if we fulfill gender-based ideals.[62] The history of sex we have inherited in the United States makes the human construction of this idolatry more than clear.

But the doctrine of justification teaches that we are freed from this bondage. And therefore, so are our images and language for God freed from this bondage of the binary because holding God in a gender-based binary—that is, God only as Father, Jesus only as Son, God acting "masculine," and Jesus always portrayed as a man—gets in the way of gospel proclamation. Androcentric images and language for the Triune God can disrupt evangelism. Instead, as I continue to say, we need language and images for God of all genders.

Proclaiming the God of all genders and no gender is evangelical. This wide range of images and language proclaims exactly what we need—freedom. We are freed from the false bondage of the gender binary. We are freed from the false bondage of androcentric religious language. Instead, we are bound to God and freed to take care of all of God's creation, including people in our great diversity. From a theological perspective, language for God simply must be freed from the false bondage of exclusively or even mostly male-identified language. The same is true for all the language for God and the images of a white Father and white Son.

Conclusion

Faith and idolatry go together for Luther. Like so much of what he thought and wrote about, faith and idolatry are a paradox and are similar. They are connected because they both have to do with the heart. Faith is full trust in our hearts in God; idolatry is full trust in our hearts in anything else. As Luther wrote, "If the heart is filled, then also the eyes and ears, mouth and nose, body and soul, and all members must be filled. For the way the heart behaves, so all members behave and act, and each and every thing you do is nothing but an expression of the praise and thanks to God."[63] I think the Lutheran theological tradition, through its orienting evangelical and theological priorities of the Reformation, empowers Christians to make faithful use of inclusive and expansive language and images for God. To be Lutheran is to be evangelical so that the gospel is clearly heard. This means that inclusive and expansive language is at the heart of what it means to be Lutheran. We proclaim the gospel not in androcentric language but in *new* old language. Even as Luther reflected theologically on experience—on lived life—and developed volumes upon volumes of theology, he urged Christians to stay in relationship with Scripture. As you might anticipate, in the final chapter, we return to Scripture, the Word of God, through which God disrupts and affirms. We find in it some *new* old language for God, who is for us.

6 Transformative Theology
God for Us

You cannot, at the same time,
mount two horses

You cannot, at the same time,
bend two bows

You cannot, at the same time,
serve two masters
—John Dominic Crossan, *The Essential Jesus*,
based on Gospel of Thomas 47:2

Friends, I beg you, become as I am, for I also have become as you are.
—Galatians 4:12

As much as I think it is inspiring to learn from and argue with Luther's theology, I know he would urge us as people of faith back to Scripture. Luther's teachings and insights flow from Scripture, including the conviction that the heart is the seat of faith and the theological paradoxes I mentioned in the previous chapter (law and gospel, the Word as proclaimed and visible, and bondage and freedom). These ideas, I have shown, can serve as a compass to support inclusive and expansive language for God from a Lutheran perspective. Luther applied the insights he gained from his study of some Scriptures to interpret other Scriptures.[1] Once again, this is what it means from a Lutheran perspective to interpret Scripture with Scripture. The key focus of Scripture, for Luther, was the gospel, the preaching of Christ *for us*. The question in this chapter is, Can we find the proclamation of the gospel in Scripture in language and images that are multigendered?

As the Word opened Luther's heart to renewed and deeper faith, Scripture can do the same to us. Sometimes this happens through personal devotional readings of Scripture, but Lutherans also trust God's gifts of a wide range of disciplines, from science to the arts to linguistics. As Luther might put it, God is the source of our abilities, so we put them to good use in faith seeking understanding. In this chapter, I offer some insights on biblical texts that disrupt and affirm how we might think about sex and gender related to God and ourselves as humans in ways that evangelize by proclaiming Christ for us. What we find in Scripture can form us in faith beyond patriarchy. God is our Mother, and she frees us from the bondage of sin, including the ways we place God and ourselves as humans in a binary of sex and gender and race with high and low positions in a hierarchy.

But how do we get to the confession that God is our Mother? It comes from careful study of Scripture. Luther was no stranger to the contextual responsibilities of translation and interpretation, which also ought to influence preaching.[2] Finding himself in conflict with any number of critics, Luther wrote regularly about translating the biblical languages but perhaps most hilariously in an open letter in 1530. Some critics thought that too much of Luther's own agenda showed up in his translations, but Luther called them "jackasses" and stressed how important it was to take into account people's whole lives when translating. Translators and interpreters of Scripture need to pay attention to how others talk, Luther wrote, and "must watch their mouth and be guided by their language," whether they are farmers, parents, entrepreneurs, or children.[3] Luther wanted to make sure that translators and interpreters of Scripture get behind the biblical text and understand that text in order to speak effectively to all manner of people.

Preaching, rooted in Scripture, is one way people receive the gospel. Luther explained that the effect of preaching is to bestow Christ as gift: "This is the great fire of the love of God for us, whereby the heart and conscience become happy, secure, and content. This is what preaching the Christian faith means."[4] I want all people to experience this fire of love and not be compelled to leave the church because this fire is squelched by androcentric language. This is what I want for those who cry during worship or hunger for a gospel they cannot hear. Thinking critically about Scripture and the language we use to proclaim the gospel clearly affects how we proclaim good news to one another. What we find in Scripture is that sex and gender "rules" and messages about God, humans, and even Jesus are sometimes disrupted and transgressed, affording us further confidence that multigendered language and images for God are scripturally faithful.

Gendered Lawlessness

We have established how the Lutheran doctrine of justification by grace through faith empowers Christians to use inclusive and expansive language for the three persons of the Trinity. To understand justification with further depth and nuance and to grasp the connections to sex and gender, we turn to Paul's letter to the Galatians. Paul carried out his mission of proclaiming the gospel within the wider context of the Roman Empire. Many biblical scholars interpret the Bible by taking into account Rome's imperial power, the predominant force in the days of Jesus and Paul. This dynamic of imperial power helps underscore the scriptural faithfulness of inclusive and expansive language for God because the way Rome created and used gendered images of who was justified (lawful) still endures today.

Rome was relentless. Rome began as a city-state, and it eventually occupied most of what is now the Italian Peninsula. Eventually, Roman emperors conquered, vanquished, and ruled many nations, including the Gauls (also known as the Galatians) in 52 BCE. Nearly a century later, Paul founded a community of followers of Jesus in Galatia among people long considered barbarians.[5]

In his letter to the Galatians, Paul declares, "Yet we know that a person is justified [also translated as 'reckoned as righteous'] not by the works of the law but through faith in Jesus Christ [also translated as 'the faith of Jesus Christ']. And we have come to believe in Christ Jesus, so that we might be justified by faith in Christ [also translated as 'the faith of Christ'], and not by doing the works of the law, because no one will be justified by the works of the law" (2:16). For Paul, God's justification in Christ disrupted the power of the Roman Empire, which was violently male dominated, male identified, and male centered. God acted in Jesus to offer a new vision and way of life beyond a masculinized empire that was violent and violently protected.

In subjugating nation after nation, Rome used the force of the military and replaced local governments with Roman colonial rule. In other words, they violently subjugated people and then established their own version of cities in the occupied territories and coerced the colonized people of these conquered nations to adhere to the Roman rules for identity. If needed, Rome enforced this identity violently.

As I explained in chapter 3, Rome was like a rooster, a cock, a violent symbol of masculinity. Roman coins, public sculptures, military wear, and drinkware valorized the male emperors for their power. The defeated nations were personified as feminine, weak men and as subdued women. The portrayals of victory and defeat are gendered, racialized, and sexualized.

One particularly public representation of Rome's patriarchal violence was the Sebasteion in the city of Aphrodisias in Asia Minor. The temple depicts scenes of Roman emperors defeating feminized nations. In one scene, the Roman emperor Claudius is a naked muscular soldier pulling back the hair of a defeated woman, Britannia, who is trapped on the ground with torn clothing, writhing to set herself free.

Imagine the president of the United States portrayed as a buff soldier about to rape a defeated woman on the ground, personified as, say, Japan just after World War II. Now imagine the United States placing that statue in the town square in, say, Hiroshima, Nagasaki, or Tokyo. The point of this visual representation was humiliation told through sexualized and gendered power.

But it was also racialized.[6] The carving of Emperor Claudius defeating Britannia looked out over an arc of porticoes, each of which had an ethnic-specific face of a defeated nation portrayed as a woman. The message was clear: Rome ruled, and all these other nations were nothing but racialized women to Rome.[7]

New Testament scholars in empire-critical studies note that "the law" of Rome relied on an ideal that the "Self" is always better and higher than the "Other." Romans were "up" and "in"; people outside of Roman law were "down" and "out." Roman law naturally included actual laws, but more importantly, it involved Roman ideals of who was righteous and who was unrighteous—who was, in fact, justified and unjustified. Roman colonialism forced the conquered

Figure 6.1. The emperor defeating Britannia, the imperial reliefs from the Sebasteion at Aphrodisias, Karacasu, Aydın Province, Turkey. Ayhan Altun / Alamy Stock Photo.

nations to adopt Roman ways and give their allegiance to the conquering, powerful nation.

Scholars like Brigitte Kahl and Davina C. Lopez describe how this message was repeated in visual depictions throughout the Roman Empire. The ideals of Roman masculinity and coercion were part of this identity. The power and value of Roman law depended on the good news, benefaction, and salvation of the Roman order. The empire's version of good news was that colonized peoples could be "justified" through Roman law by submission to it.[8] The Roman cosmos had Caesar ruling as father and son of (a) god, and Rome's good news was that when you participated in Rome's law, you received benefits from the emperor and from Rome. Roman order—the law of Rome—required people to place their own needs above the needs of others.[9] The Self was higher and better than the Other.

One large public example of this kind of participation in Roman law was the arena, where an audience gathered to cheer for the death of an Other in contests of mortal combat. The persons sent into the ring, according to Roman values, were deemed to be of lesser human value and therefore were expendable or even deserved to die. Spectators then could safely participate in cheering on the death of these "lesser" ones. Rome wanted conquered nations to believe that the people who died deserved it, including the colonized persons' own family, friends, and peers. Visual representations made it seem normal—"only natural"—that it was righteous for certain people to die.[10]

Rome also employed crucifixion to "righteously" kill Others. The cross was used as a visual deterrent to keep subjects in line with Rome's law. People were judged either lawful or lawless, considered justified or unjustified by Roman ideals. In Roman culture, one was in or out, of high status or of low status.

The history of the meaning of sex and gender followed this same pattern of in or out and high or low status. Remember, the "law" in one-sex and two-sex worldviews is that males are always and "naturally" up and in. The "law" of these worldviews is that males are more legitimate. Although we might think we do not operate this way in the twenty-first century, there are civic laws that support this hierarchy[11] and religious "laws" that embrace this hierarchy.[12] For instance, due to historic federal restrictions on tribal law, non–American Indian men who rape American Indian women and girls on tribal lands cannot be prosecuted easily. Or consider that the majority of Christians worldwide belong to church bodies that officially teach that wives should obey and follow husbands. A similar dynamic is at work in language and images for God. In this framework of who is high and who is low, who is legitimate and who is illegitimate, female-identified language for God may seem illegitimate.

Another similarity between the ancient Roman context and ours deals with suffering and death and who "deserves" it. For example, people who endure sexual violence are often questioned about or judged based on their clothing, behavior, or sexual, gender, or racial identity. The judgment that rings through this kind of questioning is that this violated person somehow got what was coming to them. This happens often to Black and brown women or people society has generally labeled as lower status.

Another "righteous" death occurs with the misuse of language. When this ideal of Self over Other pervades our hearts, we can end up thinking of sex and gender as being rooted in a power formation. Our culture is still growing out of this and into something new.

But the default position favors the idea that being "righteous" or "unrighteous" is still based primarily on sex and gender. It is everywhere in how we debate identities, how we deal with sexualized violence, and how we think about language for God. What is apparent to me is that the "law" that some are "higher" than others rules reactions to feminine and female-identified language for God. Somehow, the thinking goes, "*she* just cannot be." Scripture, however, turns us to a new vision.

Gender Disruption in Christian Identity

Returning to Paul, we see a figure whose message went against Roman ideals. Empire-critical scholars point out that Paul's arguments against law as the means of righteousness might have more to do with the acute crisis the Roman Empire created for its occupied territories than with Paul's arguments against Judaism, the tradition of his birth. The letter to the Galatians, when put in conversation with history, reveals sex and gender disruptions. Some compelling clues in the letter to the Galatians contribute to what I think are scriptural reasons for inclusive and expansive language.

Paul provokes the Galatians to be lawless by disrupting identity markers such as the practice of circumcision.[13] Paul refers to Titus, his coworker in Christ, who "was not compelled to be circumcised, though he was a Greek" (Gal 2:3). Followers of Jesus who had practiced the circumcision tradition in Judaism were clearly nervous about this kind of arrangement. Paul relates that some disciples had infiltrated the Galatian church and tried to get Gentile followers of Jesus to be circumcised. After greeting the Galatians and establishing that he preaches the true gospel of Christ, he turns quickly to this issue of circumcision.

Rome had laws about identities and about worship. As outlined in chapter 2, all conquered nations were supposed to worship Caesar, their newly adopted father of Rome. Conquered nations were the new children of the emperor. But there is even more to the story that we need to know. Perhaps because they came from an old and venerated religion, Jews were spared this edict. They were allowed to worship the God of Israel instead of Caesar. The Temple in Jerusalem still stood in Jesus's day and during the years of

Paul's ministry. Though Roman soldiers were often in the temple environs as a reminder of who was really in control, Jews could worship their God, in Jerusalem and farther afield. They were allowed to a certain extent to go about "business as usual." Jewish people also continued the religious practice of circumcision. Jesus and his male disciples would have been circumcised according to custom.

But here is the clash: Gentiles, by custom, did not circumcise male babies. This part of the ancient world had basically three types of bodies: circumcised (Jewish) males, uncircumcised (Gentile) males, and all others (women, girls, eunuchs—and other bodies).[14] A fierce debate arose among Jesus's followers regarding whether or not Gentile males should be circumcised in order to "become" Jewish so that they could follow Jesus. Some of the debate may have been from intra-Jewish arguments as Judaism branched and expanded with Jesus's ministry. But the Roman context reveals an entirely different layer, one that helps us think about our own bodies and language for God.

In the Roman imperial world, Paul's call to resist male circumcision in the communities following Jesus was both political and religious resistance. Jewish people were allowed to worship a god other than Caesar, and Jewish males were allowed to retain religious identity in the Roman Empire because of circumcision. In this context, Paul calls for yet another identity, one outside of Rome's power, one in which distinctions based on race, gender, or prior religion no longer define identity. Recall Paul's famous proclamation: "There is no longer Jew or Greek, there is no longer slave or free, there is no longer male and female; for all of you are one in Christ Jesus" (Gal 3:28). In chapter 2, we saw how Paul's preaching dethroned the Roman emperor as divine father. Reading more deeply, we now see how Paul's preaching also disrupted sex and gender rules or expectations.

Uncircumcised Galatians who worshipped the God of Israel, the God of Jesus, were deemed out of order. They embodied a kind of lawlessness. Gentile communities that did not circumcise their males and yet worshipped anyone other than Caesar rejected the identity markers that defined Roman culture and religion. Paul then closes his letter to the Galatians by saying, "For neither circumcision nor uncircumcision is anything; but a new creation is everything! As for those who will follow this rule—peace be upon them, and mercy, and upon the Israel of God" (6:15–16). Paul is not just obsessed with male anatomy; he proclaims that lawfulness—righteousness—belongs outside of the gender- and sex-based ideals of power that Rome operated within. He likewise proclaims righteousness outside of an ethnic hierarchy because the Galatians were long considered unruly ethnic Others. As Roman subjects, the Galatians would be "adopted" by their new Roman imperial father, Caesar, if they became "lawful" by taking on Roman ideals. The Galatians had to decide what to do, and Paul is coaching them.

Paul further intervenes by painting himself as a mother in labor. Imagine this image of Paul standing next to the typical statue of the emperor with rippling muscles bulging under his breastplate—the transgender Paul, crouched in labor, fluids flowing from her body, next to the Roman soldier who is twice as big. The image of Paul is intended to paint a different reality. Here is gospel! Paul proclaims a gospel of radical solidarity, Davina Lopez points out, through his motherhood.[15] Mother Paul wrote, "Friends, I beg you, become as I am, for I also have become as you are. . . . My little children, for whom I am again in the pain of childbirth until Christ is formed in you, I wish I were present with you now and could change my tone, for I am perplexed about you" (Gal 4:12, 19–20). Paul speaks and performs as a mother suffering in labor as her body heaves in contractions. Perhaps nothing could be lower in the Roman Empire—a subjugated pregnant female body in labor. But Paul is claiming that *as* a laboring mother about to give birth, he is outside the identity and the law of Rome. And remember what happens when you go against the law of Rome, when you are not righteous according to the empire—you risk being crucified. Paul joins the Galatians from below and risks that future.

Paul is proclaiming this resistance to imperial law and proclaiming a new creation in Christ by queering Self. As Lopez writes, most scholars of the past have themselves labored to prove Paul's manliness in relation to Paul's "provocative (trans)gendered image," which Lopez thinks "should just be 'sat with' in its complexity."[16] The identity Paul claims, in fact, fits a scriptural tradition of Israel suffering in labor during exile and awaiting restoration and God's call to serve all nations. About Paul's context, Lopez writes, "Paul's fertility with the Galatians is born of the physical pain and struggle of care and support among the conquered,"[17] in contrast to the racially preferential and controlled fertility and birth when Rome plunders and rapes the nations.

Just like Sunday school lessons taught, Paul went from proud man on his high horse, a manly man like the Romans, to a humble servant of Christ, a girly man to Romans: "You have heard, no doubt, of my earlier life in Judaism. I was violently persecuting the church of God and was trying to destroy it. I advanced in Judaism beyond many among my people of the same age, for I was far more zealous for the traditions of my ancestors" (Gal 1:13–14). But we usually miss this last part: Paul identifies with the sex and gender that is lowest, that is the target of control and death, and he proclaims from this lowest position, like a woman in labor.[18] His beaten body bears the marks of Christ, of faithfulness to Christ (6:17). He has become like the conquered and urges the Galatians to become the same. When Paul calls for the Galatians to "become as I am" (4:12), Lopez argues that "Paul means giving up the dynamics of domination symbolized by impenetrable imperial masculinity, unveiling a larger umbrella of patriarchal power relationships." Paul's masculinity becomes nondominant.[19]

From this low position, Paul calls the nations to the true God. In the noise of the empire, Paul declares a different cosmic order. As explained in chapter 2, the ancient world out of Greece and Rome imagined a great cosmic hierarchy, with gods at the top, privileged and free men next, followed by all others in descending order. In this cosmic order, only free men who were fathers had ideas and generated legitimate sons. For Rome, the emperor was a god at the top of that cosmic hierarchy. The emperor of the violently masculinized Roman Empire was presumed to be the god of the nations. As we have seen through the letter to the Galatians, this false god is male dominated, male identified, and male centered. Rome's offer of salvation was tied to the peace of Rome, the Pax Romana. Conquered nations lived under this promise of protection as long as those conquered lived by Roman law.

Rooted in the Jewish tradition and his heritage of anti-idolatry, Paul proclaims resurrection, exodus, and new creation through a different Father, the God of Israel. To receive this gospel, people in Roman colonies needed the true God to have a title that challenged the false god, the false father. So Paul shows the contrast in fathers—and he also shows the contrast in justification. Justification comes from God's love through Christ. In turn, the followers of Jesus Christ are called to love others without the self-aggrandizement of selfishness. This is a love that serves others by paying attention to their needs. This upends and disrupts the values of the gendered, racialized, and sexualized Roman Empire. It is the kind of love that can get the followers of Jesus Christ crucified—because it challenges Roman law.

Paul declares freedom in Christ in the horizontal fashion of a laboring mother rather than in a vertical hierarchy of the father ideology of Rome.[20] Paul is part of the messianic movement that challenged idols in favor of the true God, the one who is for us, the God Luther describes as the God of promise, the Word as womb. In other words, empire-critical scholarship that delves into the context of the New Testament pulls the curtain back on this other crucial aspect of language for God: the good news of Jesus, the gospel Paul preached, the Word Luther describes as simultaneously transformative and gender ambiguous challenges patriarchal gender constructions. What else do we know about the God of all creation in Scripture? And how will this help us faithfully include feminine and queer language and images for God? We now turn to a passage of Scripture that disrupts gendered expectations about God's character.

Gender Disruption in God's Character

Deuteronomy might not be a book of the Bible you ordinarily go to when you think about inclusive and expansive language for God, but it holds an incredible image of God as a bird that is difficult to distinguish by sex. Scholars think Deuteronomy was written long after Moses's death and the Israelite people's entrance into a new land after being in the desert for forty years. Biblical scholar Carolyn Pressler points out that Deuteronomy was likely written to help King Josiah (640–609 BCE) oppose idolatry and centralize worship in Judah.[21] In a way, it was written to remember the past and to anticipate the future.[22] Although Luther did not have the same access to historical tools as we do today, he interpreted the laws and poetry of Deuteronomy alike as Moses's drive toward faith. The whole book, Luther wrote, "contains nothing else than faith toward God and love toward one's neighbor, for all of the laws of God come to that."[23] What I find compelling in thinking about language for God and how Scripture disrupts and affirms our expectations about God comes in the final chapters of Deuteronomy, especially in Moses's farewell speech.

In Deuteronomy 32:6, God is referred to as a father: "Is not he your father, who created you, who made you and established you?" Here we have an ancient expression of the one-sex worldview of reproduction—that fathers alone give the substance or are the source for another human being. Verses 7 to 9 continue the image of God as the generating and ruling father. Verse 8 refers to God as the Most High (*Elyon* in Hebrew), a name that seems to support a one-sex worldview of God ruling. One commentary states that the title *Elyon* suggests "the executive of the divine assembly," which has subordinate gods, "literally, 'sons of God.'"[24] Actual men are just below these "sons of God." But in verse 10, ideas about God start to be disrupted. God cares for people "as the apple of his eye," drawing an intimate expression of God's loyalty.

Then the understanding of God as predominantly or exclusively male or masculine is put on its head. In particular, verses 11–12 seem to introduce sex and gender ambiguity to understand God. Here we find an image of God as a bird. The word in Hebrew is *nesher*. One translation reads, "As a *nesher* stirs up its nest, flutters over its young, spreads out its wings, takes them, bears them on its pinions; So did God guide them, and there was no strange god with them."[25] For a long time, translators thought people would cringe or otherwise not connect with what a *nesher* is, so they called it an eagle. It is actually a griffon vulture. In the midst of verses that seem to communicate male-identified divine anger, God is a large bird that is known for consuming decaying flesh. It is a cleaner and purifier.

For English readers to shift away from the image of God as an eagle might take some work. Eagles are used to picture empires. Eagles topped Roman standards. Ancient carvings show caricatures of peoples conquered by Rome having a hard time holding up the eagle standard. The Third Reich also used eagles to symbolize their power on posters, stamps, and all manner of insignia. The eagle is also a symbol for the United States. The eagle seems royal. But this bird, the griffon vulture, symbolizes something different. Vultures keep disease at bay by eating what is deadly to living creatures—the dead.[26] God as vulture helps explain the essential necessity of God for life by keeping disease at bay and eating what is dangerous, even what is deadly.

And even more important to my point regarding God's character in Deuteronomy is that it is difficult to tell griffon vultures apart by sex. God as griffon vulture disrupts any idea that God is male identified because to the naked eye, griffon vultures are nearly indistinguishable in size, weight, and color. These vultures are enormous, with wingspans over six and a half feet. They have the same fringes of brown feathers. Their features are so similar that scientists usually must rely on DNA testing to determine the sex of a particular bird. But even then, they have found, the tests are not always accurate.[27] God as griffon vulture gives a picture of God of all sexes and genders. People living in the ancient Middle East would have known this because they saw these birds themselves and could have seen that they were all similar. Yet this sex and gender disruption is not only in looks but also in character.

One study concludes that griffon vultures have no detectable competitive differences based on sex.[28] They often fly together[29] and bond through nest building, usually up in the crags of high rock formations.[30] As coparents, they protect the vulnerable with what we might call devotion, taking turns for almost two months to incubate the one egg the female lays. The chick is born very weak and tiny, around six ounces. At four months, the little griffon vulture has just begun to grow feathers and is still cared for by both parents because it is not yet independent.[31] God in this verse is devoted parent.

In a fascinating continued sex and gender reversal, God is maternal in Deuteronomy 32:18: "You were unmindful of the Rock that bore you; you forgot the God who gave you birth." Although a rock is not typically a maternal reference, the nonsentient status of a rock further disrupts our expectations about God. More compelling, however, is the verb in this verse. The Hebrew verb for "gave you birth" is translated literally as "writhed in travail" in labor.[32] Here is another instance in which a literal translation matters for inclusive and expansive language because it broadens the image of God.

The wording in the verses in chapter 32 moves from *father* to *devoted parent* to *mother*. Scripture affirms God's love for us, even while it disrupts our expectations of who God is through these all-encompassing images of sex and gender identity for God. Galatians and Deuteronomy offer images of humans and God that are not masculine or feminine but are both. Looking further into the Scriptures, we also find examples of sex and gender being reversed or transgressed.

Human and Divine Gender Transgression

The book of Jeremiah and the Gospel of John each hold images of gender transgression or reversal. Although their texts, characters, and forms of gender reversals are different, I think they each disrupt idolizing masculinity over and against femininity and draw subtle yet powerful portraits of God's future unhinged from a gender-based binary or hierarchy.

The book of Jeremiah was written over the course of many years while Judah suffered repeated invasions, wars, and displacements. The book fuses history with symbols and storytelling to make sense of the people's cross-generational trauma. When read as a whole, scholars agree that the book was meant to help people interpret their multilayered tragedies, remember who they are as God's people, and discern the future God promises them. Jeremiah's life narrated throughout the book mirrors Judah's experiences as a nation suffering loss, seeking identity, and discerning God's future for them.[33]

Scholars disagree, however, on how to make sense of the many uses and disruptions of gender. Lutheran biblical scholar Corrine Carvalho interprets Jeremiah with a focus on God's promise and through queer theory, which assesses gender as a social construction.[34] She provides three central insights tied to gender transgression and reversal: about God, about the prophet, and about promised restoration in God.

The first insight is about war and God. Just as imperial Rome often used images of subdued nations as women, the book of Jeremiah describes defeated men as vulnerable women. The king of Judah is a raped woman (13:20–27). Men vanquished in battle are pregnant women grabbing their bellies in the throes of labor (30:6). The nation understands its vulnerability and defeat through female personification, what Carvalho calls gender-bending in war. As I explained above, hundreds of years after Jeremiah was written, Rome continued to use this personification, but from the victors' viewpoint, as the manly men defeating the girly men. Carvalho adds to this understanding of gender-bending in war. She points out that God is portrayed like a divinity of Assyria. To detect this scriptural gender-bending about God, we need historical information.

Babylon was one of the nations that repeatedly defeated Judah. The people of Assyria, a nation northwest of Babylon, worshipped Ishtar. Carvalho explains that "Ishtar was a gender-bending deity" who was embodied in transgender priests and who spoke through prophets who did not conform to the expectations of how to be masculine or feminine.[35] Ishtar as a warrior subverted "the gendered rhetoric of the male victor" that was normal in that region.[36] Now here is the interesting thing. Most of us who read the Bible think that the images of Yahweh in battle and as a warrior belong just to the God of Israel—and that the God of Israel is a male god. Not so, Carvalho points out, because "many of these images have closer parallels to the kind of violence perpetrated by Ishtar." She concludes, "Yahweh's gender in war, even in the book of Jeremiah, is not as stable as often assumed."[37] The God of Israel is described similarly to how gender-bending Ishtar was described.

The second insight Carvalho offers is about the prophet Jeremiah. Just like God's gender is reversed in the book of Jeremiah, so is the prophet's. God interferes with Jeremiah's gender performance as an acceptable man. The more Jeremiah trusts God, the more his "normal" manliness is acutely undone. For example, Carvalho points out, Jeremiah weeps like a woman who wept professionally for and within communities (13:17). God tells Jeremiah not to marry, have children, or go to people's funerals, all activities of an honorable man (16:1–5). In this text, closeness to God means distance from acceptable gender performance. And throughout chapters 11–20, Jeremiah laments and accuses God of seduction and deception. As Carvalho explains, Jeremiah "becomes functionally impotent as a symbol of God's exclusive claim on him."[38] God is described in a gender-ambiguous way because Yahweh is talked about in the same way as Ishtar, a gender-bending divinity, but also the prophet's closeness to God results in transgressing the normal activities of an acceptable man. Carvalho points out that something theological is said through gender reversal. Jeremiah has no access to gender performance as a man because God cut him off from it. Carvalho concludes that God provokes and sustains social upheaval.[39] But why?

The third insight is the way the text portrays God's promised restoration through gender reversal. Although numerous passages in the book of Jeremiah reinforce gender expectations in a patriarchal society, Carvalho focuses on a key verse to interpret the text as a whole (31:22). In this verse, a woman will surround a man. The word for "surround" can also mean "encompass" and can carry stereotypical feminine (with comfort or in sex) or masculine (in warrior protection) characteristics. This verse seems to offer a paradox for gendered expectations. For Carvalho, this verse is a key to the rest of the text because it shows that gender instability is part of social destruction and part of the new world to which the book points. This hoped-for future is God's promise.[40] Carvalho's interpretation suggests that God brings new order through boundary transgression. Queering, then, is part of God's good work in the world, which we see in how the community of Judah saw itself, Jeremiah's relationship with God, and God's self-revelation.

The queering of gender identity is also found in the Gospel of John (13:1–20), which tells of Jesus washing the disciples' feet. A common interpretation of this foot washing is that Jesus is humiliating himself, making himself the servant. Servants, after all, were largely responsible for washing their masters' feet. Sometimes students were too. Biblical scholar Sandra M. Schneiders claims that Jesus models service, but the form of service Jesus embodies in this text is one of friendship, in which equals serve one another simply for the good of the other. This kind of service is not the same as unequal forms of service based on different degrees of power, such as between an employee and employer or a child and a parent. Instead, in the Gospel of John, service is between equals, which Jesus symbolizes by washing disciples' feet. As she emphasizes, Jesus calls his disciples *friends*, not servants (15:15).

Yet in John's version of the foot-washing story, Jesus's gender is disrupted or transgressed. Biblical scholars explain that most often, female slaves and Jewish wives were responsible for washing masters' and husbands' feet. Foot washing may have symbolized a gender-based role of intimacy or service. It would have been culturally outrageous for free men to wash the feet of women and slaves. Customs about who washed whose feet were strictly kept.[41]

Jesus's action breaks from community rules and norms. Some scholars believe he is doing this using gender-based symbolism. The towel Jesus put on his waist was likely the symbol of those who washed other people's feet.[42] It is interesting to think about Peter's shock when Jesus offers to wash his feet in this possible gender transgression. Jesus is not only making himself equal to the disciples by washing their feet but also making females equal to males, all friends of God.

Jesus takes on the symbol of gender-based service in order to reveal friendship in God and takes on the status of the gendered lowest in a worldview of male over female. Jesus as male and female starts to make symbolic sense. To think about this further, we return to an image from the introduction to this book. Jesus himself talks directly about a twin gendered identity, one that we might not so readily remember because, as I pointed out already, the tradition has not emphasized it. Through parable, Jesus disrupts androcentric imagery for who he is as the Christ.

Jesus the Good Householder

In the introduction, I asked how Christians and Christian faith might change if the parable of the Good Householder in Luke 15:8–10 were in churches and hearts and liturgies nearly as often as the Good Shepherd is. The Good Householder is not the only feminine image for Jesus or God in the Bible, but for now, it is where we will return for three simple reasons: it is largely overlooked as language and image for Jesus, its gender-disrupting importance has been largely invisible to the Christian tradition, and it offers fresh insight into language and images for God from all genders. Recall that the Good Householder is the woman who tears her house apart to find her tenth coin that rolled away, out of sight. Along with the story of the Good Shepherd, Jesus tells the story about her to explain why he does what he does.

When my godmother retired from ministry, friends in the congregation commissioned a small stained glass window of the woman searching for the coin for her farewell gift. It's lovely. And I know it means so much to my godmother. But what if the image of the Good Householder took up space among all the male-identified figures, both in our chancels and in our hearts? It might be that this is what the writer of Luke was doing—disrupting gender-based messages or rules.

The Gospels do not record Jesus saying, "I am the Good Householder."[43] While true in one respect, it is possible the writer of Luke might be saying this very thing. While the Gospel of John certainly has Jesus call himself the Good Shepherd, in Luke, there are more images. At the very least, there are these twin images of a shepherd (15:3–7) and a householder (15:8–10), but there is a third story in the sequence, the landowner father with two sons (15:11–32).

Scholars cannot pinpoint when Luke was written, but most think it was in the last third of the first century. Many feminist scholars point out that Luke has more female characters than Mark and material common to both Matthew and Luke (the Q source) combined.[44] But the writer of Luke tries to present these women in acceptable forms for imperial Rome. Some scholars think Roman women were not in leadership roles and did not exercise authority like women in the Jesus movement did. But the Jesus movement was held in suspicion and accused of magic by Roman officials. Jesus's followers were seen as a threat to the family and the state. People who followed Jesus were believed to be dangerous.[45]

The Gospel of Luke can seem awfully inconsistent about women. The disciples who are women are paired up with husbands. Mary and Martha argue about kitchen service. Peter has to show up at Easter because the women tell idle tales. Can no woman in Luke be legitimate or lawful on her own? The writer of Luke has both populated the Jesus movement stories with women—and put them in their places based on cultural norms. They appear to be "safe" in Luke, some scholars argue.[46]

But are they? Given that this is a text written by a group under suspicion and under occupation, there might be more to the story—or at least more that many people in the United States would not recognize immediately. The story of the Good Householder is paired with the parable of the Good Shepherd. As biblical scholar Luise Schottroff remarks, in a world of making women invisible, the fact that she is simply in the text is remarkable.[47]

What do we know about her? The dire poverty of the woman contrasts sharply with the shepherd and the landowner father. The householder appears to have no secure food (as the shepherd presumably does) and no land (as the father does). She lives in bitter need; she needs that coin "to survive, even more than the shepherd needs his hundredth sheep."[48] Life itself depends on that lost coin, which could likely be redeemed for enough food for two days. The story is a visceral description of desperation, clearly accounted for in the details of her search. I imagine her eyes wild with need, her clothes dusty, and her hair at odds with her scarf and scalp. She tore that house apart to find the one coin.

Brigitte Kahl points out that Luke and Acts (Luke–Acts) make clear the security risk the followers of Jesus were within the Roman power structures.

The book of Luke is written to Theophilus, who Kahl notes is likely concerned; he is "somebody in a hierarchical position concerned about this
matter . . . 'security.'"[49] Jesus tells this set of parables in this context. On the
one hand, the story of the woman householder stands between two narratives
about men. In these parables, each person finds what they are looking for.
On the other hand, Luke also refers to women who were healed by Jesus and
likely were disciples but keeps them silent (8:3).

As part of the church resistance that led to the fall of the Berlin Wall in
1989, Kahl knows well the ways messages or stories are conveyed so that, on
the one hand, the listener who holds the power for life or death hears something
completely different from what, on the other hand, the resisting conversation
partner hears. The one often understands nonsense, with the other making
sense of what matters. Kahl writes with full knowledge: "Writing/speaking
under external or internal censorship almost automatically produces a kind
of text which is self-contradictory in that it 'serves two masters': the 'obedient reader' who observes the rules of the (reading) game established by the
omnipresent imaginary or real 'censor,' and the 'subversive reader' who reads
'between the lines,' searching the 'compromise' of the text for counter-readings
and hidden or coded information."[50] This, she demonstrates, is a likely scriptural principle in Luke–Acts and one that I think helps us through its gender
disruption to understand inclusive language for God as scripturally faithful.

In this Gospel, the narrator begins by saying they will tell things to
Theophilus from the beginning. Kahl points out that this framework echoes
Genesis and is no small matter. The remarkable feature of the story told to a
man who was nervous about what the Jesus movement means to the Roman
Empire is that "the beginning" in Luke is not in the normal manner of kings
and battles and such, as Rome would value. Instead, the beginning of the
story about Jesus is about two women and two children: "But now, the beginning of the time of God's promise is posited most dramatically in a time ros-
ter that is gynocentric."[51] There is a reorientation to time that might be missed
by a listener with power. Reading between the lines, she notes, the story takes
away time from the patriarch, the pater familias Zechariah.

Zechariah's muteness from not believing God, Kahl points out, underscores the way, instead, two women and two babies foreground the entire
book of Luke. "The patriarchal house of Zechariah, as the nucleus of the

social structure of domination," is reordered by God's promised future. In the Magnificat, Mary gives voice to a radical hope "for justice and for a world without domination and submission, without shortage and surplus. Messianic time has begun."[52] With this reorientation of reading at work, the householder is terribly important—central, even—for the people speaking above and beyond the listeners who have the power to kill or to let live.

Lutheran biblical scholar Carol Schersten LaHurd points out that part of the problem has been the Christian tradition's theological interpretation of the twin stories.[53] The woman is not weak in her own context of household and survival, even, I think, if imperial readers would have read her as weak.

The shepherd, the householder, and the landowner father, LaHurd writes, each have the power to complete what is missing from something—the flock, the treasury, or family relations.[54] Although she is in a different place socially, she does have power to restore what is sorely missing and needed. In fact, of all three figures, she is the one who represents the critical need to recover what is lost in order to survive.

There is an intimacy of mutuality and interconnectedness, oddly enough, between the woman and the coin. If she did not recover the coin, she would likely die prematurely, yet the other two characters who recover something or someone do not appear to be veering toward premature death. Their needs to recover what is lost are less dire for survival, even if tragic in the loss of a child.

The lowly woman is a form of the Messiah, even as the Good Shepherd is a form of the Messiah. Read from the perspective of resistance, which Kahl suggests for reading Luke–Acts, the householder is a complex figure, representing the image of God and the image of the Messiah, Jesus the Christ. You might wonder about this disruption of our expectations about God and gender.

Further reflection on part of the parable brings us to another image of God. These are eschatological images. Eschatology is theological reflection about the end of time or the future anticipated in God. Throughout history, many Christians have described the end-times as scary, full of fear, and violently disruptive. I think back to the man with the banner shouting on a Chicago street.

While no human can know the future, a Lutheran perspective is oriented through Christ. This means that the future is first rooted in God's promise of grace and mercy through faith in Jesus Christ. Lutherans focus on God's surprising love for us by being human with us in Jesus Christ. God joins us in both sorrow and joy. Lutherans also focus on how God justifies the seams of our lives in healing and beauty by stepping into death itself. The future, like the past and present, is in God's hands. We know about this through the shocking joy of the women at the tomb. But if we pay attention to reading the parable of the woman and the lost coin as communication between resisters in an empire of gender hierarchy and violence, we find another image of God, that of a party of women rejoicing.

Both the Good Shepherd and the Good Householder parables have parties. After the shepherd retrieves the lost sheep and after the woman finds the lost coin, they each call together neighbors and have a party. Schottroff thinks the parties in the twin stories show that the gatherings themselves are images of God because "joy must be shared." Women neighbors might have had some communal food, sharing bits with one another to make a feast of sorts. They likely sang and chatted.[55] Likely the men who joined the shepherd partied similarly. The story of the landowner father and his two sons also ends with a party. All three parables, in fact, close with images of healing and rejoicing. In these stories, rather than the future holding death and destruction, we come to the eschatological vision of parties as the foretaste of God's promise. We can add women partying to our vision of God *for us*.

The image of God is a group of women friends partying. Jesus is the Good Householder, the woman who searched for the lost coin. And we are her treasure, her life, for as Saint Augustine is said to have declared, "Holy Divinity has lost her money, and it is us!" This is the Word of God, the promise made to all. She is the God *for us*.

Conclusion

May the grace of Jesus Christ, the love of God, and the communion of
the Holy Spirit be with all of us.

—based on 2 Corinthians 13:13

I hope, through this book, that I have stressed my conviction that Lutherans and other Christians need to proclaim the grace of God in feminine
language—and in all genders simultaneously. I say this because the gospel is
being lost for some people because of androcentric language and images. I say
this also because I believe our Lutheran traditions provide theological and
scriptural reasons for using feminine language and images.

By delving into history, biblical studies, and contemporary theology in
relationship to Martin Luther's reforming theological insights and his own
life, I showed patterns and insights that help Christians embrace language and
images for God that are feminine, masculine, and neutral and at the same time
scripturally, evangelically, and theologically faithful. Just as Luther taught that
God is *for us* in Word and sacrament, we can know God for us through multigendered language and images so that we might declare, "May the grace of
Jesus Christ, God's Child; the love of God our Mother; and the power of the
Holy Spirit, breath of life, be with us all," or "May the grace of our Mother
Jesus Christ, the love of God our Father, and the power of the Holy Spirit be
with us all and nourish us in the womb of the Word of God."

By looking at the history of sex in one-sex and two-sex worldviews, I have shown how gendered symbols for God have historically supported patriarchy and white supremacy. This historical legacy led to understanding and treating people as "higher" and "lower," in which the "higher" people are more legitimate and the "lower" people are illegitimate. The Christian faith does not need to be beholden to this history in the language of faith, including language and images for God.

The Lutheran theological insights I have highlighted can free Christians to use multigendered language for God. Using these insights, we can faithfully affirm that patriarchy and its intersections with white supremacy and other systems of oppression are sinful. The doctrine of justification by grace through faith helps us understand God's condemnation of androcentrism. Yet this doctrine means little if, as Luther surely understood, people are not able to receive the proclamation of God's grace through Christ. If androcentric language for God interferes with the gospel, other words must be used. Luther urged preachers and biblical scholars to empathize with and respond to the lives of real people.

Luther's life also orients language for God as we seek direction. Even though a one-sex worldview prevailed in his lifetime in Germany, Luther did things that showed that his theology led to challenging the predominant or usual "rules" about sex and gender. Luther—as theologian, pastor, biblical scholar, spouse, teacher, and father—challenged the idea that females were imperfect males. The same life-giving theological reformation insights that powered and empowered Luther can continue to challenge all the ways we create uneven value and hierarchies of power, worth, vocation, and identities among people—and in language and images for God.

Luther's theological convictions serve to guide us still. Because the heart is the seat of either idolatry or faith, what serves faith must affect the heart. The heart needs to be formed and nurtured in ways that sustain faith. Luther knew this. We can faithfully use language and images that are, as he also said, necessary for faith and have the power to proclaim. The Word of God is made known through our words. Christian language and images for God must be multigendered and not androcentric. From Luther's own hand, we learn that the Word of God is paradoxical, generative, transformative, effective, and powerful and understanding of the Word is identified with no particular sex or gender but with all—and with none.

I also showed that it is scripturally faithful to proclaim the gospel and to worship the Triune God in multigendered language. Searching the Scriptures for nondominant images and themes, like listening for nondominant instruments in music, gives us further insights into God and ourselves. Scripture disrupts expectations or rules about sex and gender, which I have shown in examples from Old and New Testaments and by paying careful attention to the meaning of Paul's letter to the Galatians within the Roman Empire.

But what do you do now? Talking is helpful. By talking, I mean dialogue. How we talk about God brings up many emotions, and sometimes the conversations can be difficult. Of course, we need to be able to talk about how language for God affects us, just as I described in this book. Such dialogue includes being in conversation with biblical scholarship, church history, religious art, and more. Biblical scholars give insights not readily available, such as the image of God as griffon vulture. Church historians uncover prayers of the past, such as Saint Anselm of Canterbury's, which refers to Jesus as our Mother. Art historians study works like a carving of a pregnant Jesus crucifixion from Germany in the medieval era. When we talk together about such things, we might begin to discover new old ways to proclaim God *for us*. Try to imagine what liturgy, Bible study, and hymns are like when the Trinity is no longer the white Father in the heavens but is our Mother who loves us. Consider how to incorporate such texts into worship. Analyze your worship services and Christian education. Study. Pray. Let the God of Jesus Christ work in us all. We just might discover that She is still at work through Jesus Christ by the power of the Holy Spirit, always to be reforming the church.

Notes

Introduction

1 James Cone, *God of the Oppressed* (New York: Seabury, 1975), vi.

2 In 2011, the National Council of the Churches of Christ (NCC), to which the ELCA belongs, sponsored the initiative Words Matter. The initiative included online devotional resources and in-person workshops to raise awareness over language for God and humans and to support positive changes for gender and racial diversity in everyday and religious language.

3 See Evangelical Lutheran Church in America, *Faith, Sexism, and Justice: A Call to Action* (Chicago: Evangelical Lutheran Church in America, 2019), https://download.elca.org/ELCA%20Resource%20Repository/Faith_Sexism_Justice_Social_Statement_Adopted.pdf?_ga=2.68621905.1110212823.1631894531-1092238982.1556124288. See specifically the section "Implementing Resolutions for Faith, Sexism, and Justice: A Call to Action," 82.

4 For these insights, I thank John Dominic Crossan, *Jesus: A Revolutionary Biography* (New York: HarperSanFrancisco, 1994), 66–70.

Chapter 1: The Church and Language for God

1 Susan McArver, Convocation of Teaching Theologians of the ELCA and ELCIC (online conference, July 28, 2021).

2 See, e.g., Isabel Wilkerson, *Caste: The Origins of Our Discontents* (New York: Random House, 2020); David Grann, *Killers of the Flower Moon: The Osage Murders and the Birth of the FBI* (New York: Vintage, 2017); Danielle L. McGuire, *At the Dark End of the Street* (New York: Knopf, 2010); and Maxine Hong Kingston,

The Woman Warrior: Memoirs of a Girlhood Among Ghosts (1975; repr., London: Picador, 2015).

3 See, e.g., Loreen Maseno and Elia Shabani Mligo, *Women within Religions: Patriarchy, Feminism, and the Role of Women in Selected World Religions* (Eugene, OR: Wipf & Stock, 2019).

4 See Jimmy Carter, *A Call to Action: Women, Religion, Violence, and Power* (New York: Simon & Schuster, 2014).

5 See Melinda Gates, *The Moment of Lift: How Empowering Women Changes the World* (New York: Flatiron, 2019).

6 See "General Synod Inclusive Language," United Church of Christ, accessed September 24, 2021, https://www.ucc.org/who-we-are/about/general-synod/worship_inclusive-language_general-synod-inclusive.

7 See "Inclusive Language Resources," United Church of Christ, accessed September 24, 2021, https://www.ucc.org/what-we-do/justice-local-church-ministries/local-church/mesa-ministerial-excellence-support-and-authorization/ministers/ministers_local-church-leaders/worship_inclusive-language/worship_inclusive-language_inclusive-language-resources.

8 See Mary Frances Schjonberg and Melodie Woerman, "Convention Approves Use of Expansive-Language Version of Rite II Eucharistic Prayers," Episcopal News Service, July 12, 2018, https://www.episcopalnewsservice.org/2018/07/12/convention-approves-use-of-expansive-language-version-of-rite-ii-eucharistic-prayers.

9 The description of Lutheran history on language for God comes largely from my article, "Language: Idolatry and Evangelism," *Currents in Theology and Mission* 43, no. 3 (July 2016): 3–7, http://www.currentsjournal.org/index.php/currents/issue/view/4.

10 American Lutheran Church, Church Council Action 76.6.119, Church Council and Executive Council Minutes (TALC 8/2) (Elk Grove Village, IL: Archives of the Evangelical Lutheran Church in America, June 14–18, 1976), 84–85.

11 Gail Ramshaw Schmidt, "*De Divinis nominibus*: The Gender of God," *Worship* 56 (March 1982): 127.

12 H. Frederick Reisz Jr., "Language and God: Theological and Pastoral Issues," in *Women and Men in the Body of Christ: A Report by the Advisory Committee for the Study on Women and Men in the Body of Christ* (New York: Lutheran Church in America, 1987), 84 (emphasis in original).

13 Office of the Secretary and the Commission for Communication, *Guidelines for Inclusive Use of the English Language for Speakers, Writers and Editors* (Chicago: Evangelical Lutheran Church in America, 1989), 15.

14 Elaine Neuenfeldt, ed., *Gender Justice Policy* (Geneva: Lutheran World Federation, 2013), https://www.lutheranworld.org/sites/default/files/DTPW-WICAS _Gender_Justice.pdf. The policy is available in over twenty languages.

15 Evangelical Lutheran Church in America, *Faith, Sexism, and Justice*, 44.

16 Mary Daly, *Beyond God the Father: Toward a Philosophy of Women's Liberation* (Boston: Beacon, 1973), 19.

17 See, e.g., Carol Christ, *Rebirth of the Goddess: Finding Meaning in Feminist Spirituality* (New York: Routledge, 1997); and Mary Daly, *Gyn/Ecology: The Metaethics of Radical Freedom* (Boston: Beacon, 1978).

18 See, e.g., Elisabeth Schüssler Fiorenza, *But She Said: Feminist Practices of Biblical Interpretation* (Boston: Beacon, 1992); Jacquelyn Grant, *White Women's Christ and Black Women's Jesus: Feminist Christology and Womanist Response*, American Academy of Religion Academy Series 64, ed. Susan Thistlethwaite (Atlanta: Scholars, 1989); and Delores Williams, *Sisters in the Wilderness: The Challenges of Womanist God-Talk* (Maryknoll, NY: Orbis, 1993).

19 Brian Wren, *What Language Shall I Borrow? God-Talk in Worship: A Male Response to Feminist Theology* (New York: Crossroad, 1989), 143–70. Chapter 6 is titled "Bring Many Names," as is a hymn of the same name.

20 Elizabeth A. Johnson, *She Who Is: The Mystery of God in Feminist Theological Discourse* (New York: Crossroad, 1994).

21 Donald G. Bloesch, *The Battle for the Trinity: The Debate over Inclusive God-Language* (Ann Arbor, MI: Vine, 1985), 47, 48.

22 Bloesch, 47–54.

23 See, e.g., Bloesch, 44. Robert W. Jenson, "The Triune Name of God," in *Christian Dogmatics*, vol. 1, ed. Carl E. Braaten and Robert W. Jenson (Philadelphia: Fortress, 1984), 93–95.

24 Bloesch, *Battle for the Trinity*, 50.

25 Jenson, "Triune Name of God," 94–95.

26 Paul R. Hinlicky, *Beloved Community: Critical Dogmatics after Christendom* (Grand Rapids, MI: Eerdmans, 2015), 84.

27 Hinlicky, 85.

28 Hinlicky, 86.

29 James Cone, *The Cross and the Lynching Tree* (Maryknoll, NY: Orbis, 2011), xvi. Nota bene: Cone did not capitalize *black*.

30 See Mary J. Streufert, ed., *Transformative Lutheran Theologies: Feminist, Womanist, and Mujerista Perspectives* (Minneapolis: Fortress, 2010), esp. the introduction, 1–11.

Chapter 2: Fathers—Created Better and the Only Creators

1 "Breastfeeding State Laws," National Conference of State Legislatures, last modified August 26, 2021, https://www.ncsl.org/research/health/breastfeeding -state-laws.aspx.

2 Carly Stern, "Six Black Women Detail the Horrific Discrimination They've Faced Because of Their HAIR—Revealing How They Were FIRED from Jobs for Wearing Natural Styles, or Forced to Spend Hundreds of Dollars to Keep Their Locks Straight," *Daily Mail*, August 25, 2020, https://www.dailymail .co.uk/femail/article-8662305/Six-black-women-horrific-discrimination -faced-hair.html. See also D. Sharmin Arefin, "Is Hair Discrimination Race Discrimination?," American Bar Association, April 17, 2020, https://www .americanbar.org/groups/business_law/publications/blt/2020/05/hair -discrimination.

3 Centers for Disease Control, "Racial and Ethnic Disparities Continue in Pregnancy-Related Deaths," press release, September 5, 2019, https://www.cdc .gov/media/releases/2019/p0905-racial-ethnic-disparities-pregnancy-deaths .html.

4 See, e.g., Deanese Williams-Harris, "Racism's Toll on Black Women Includes Staggering Maternal Death Rates," *Chicago Tribune*, May 3, 2021, https://www .chicagotribune.com/living/health/ct-black-maternal-health-week-advocacy -tt-20210503-o4n6ovxlufazpbx4yype6tv6l4-story.html.

5 Although there are other streams in the worldwide history of sex and gender (and sexuality), I am focusing on what appears to be a significant historical influence on the United States and contemporary Christianity in this country.

6 For the development of the idea of intersectionality, see Kimberlé Crenshaw, "Demarginalizing the Intersection of Race and Sex: A Black Feminist Critique of Antidiscrimination Doctrine, Feminist Theory and Antiracist Politics," *University of Chicago Legal Forum* (1989): 139–167.

7 There is some debate in the literature on the history of sex. I have tried to speak as accurately as possible about this history, particularly when the his- tory described in literature relates to Christianity. See, e.g., Katharine Park with Robert A. Nye, "Destiny Is Anatomy," essay review of Thomas Laqueur, *Making Sex*, *New Republic*, February 18, 1991, 53–57.

8 See Thomas Laqueur, *Making Sex: Body and Gender from the Greeks to Freud* (Cambridge, MA: Harvard University Press, 1990), 34–35.

9 Laqueur, 8.

10 Laqueur, 26, 82.

11 See, e.g., Laqueur, 4–5, 28.

12 Laqueur, 10.

13 Laqueur, 46.

14 See, e.g., Caroline Walker Bynum, *Fragmentation and Redemption: Essays on Gender and the Human Body in Medieval Religion* (New York: Zone, 1992), 214–15.

15 See Laqueur, *Making Sex*, 36–38.

16 Laqueur, 30.

17 See Laqueur, 42.

18 Laqueur, 20.

19 See Laqueur, 6, 8, 22.

20 See Laqueur, 52–54.

21 Laqueur, 55.

22 As quoted in Laqueur, 30 (emphasis in original).

23 See Laqueur, 56–57.

24 Laqueur, 57.

25 See Laqueur, 58.

26 Laqueur, 54–55.

27 Mary Beard, *Women & Power: A Manifesto* (New York: Liveright, 2017), 97.

28 Exceptions involved defense of life, witness before martyrdom, and defense of home, children, husband, and other women. See Beard, 13, 16.

29 See Beard, 3–19.

30 See Beard, 21–30.

31 For an incisive account of how Euripides, an ancient Greek playwright and thinker, forged multifaceted critiques of power, see Paul D. Streufert, introduction to *Trojan Women*, by Euripides (Peterborough, Canada: Broadview, 2021), 9–16.

32 Laqueur, *Making Sex*, 59.

33 See Laqueur, 58.

34 Plutarch, as quoted in Laqueur, 59.

35 In contemporary Christian writing, traces of this are in the rhetoric of the Promise Keepers and in the papal encyclical *Mulieris Dignitatem*. See my "Idolatry-Critical Justification and the Foreclosed Gendered Life," in *Lutheran Identity and Political Theology*, ed. Carl-Henric Grenholm and Göran Gunner, Church of Sweden Research Series 9 (Eugene, OR: Pickwick, 2014), 134–52.

36 See Beard, *Women & Power*, 58–59.

37 See Brigitte Kahl, *Galatians Re-imagined: Reading with the Eyes of the Vanquished*, Paul in Critical Contexts (Minneapolis: Fortress, 2010), 94.

38 See Kahl, 150–51.

39 See Kahl, 183.

40 See, e.g., Kahl, 94, 184.

41 See Kahl, 182–83. For some communities under Caesar's fatherhood, the oneness of subjects' identity came together through arena spectacles, where the

emperor gave gifts to people; he gave them the "good works" of the games, the animals and humans at battle, and occasional presents and free food, randomly bestowed in the crowd, which was made into one through their common gaze at the arena and their physical and vocal participation as spectators in the gift of the pater patriae, the emperor. See Kahl, 150–51. On the point that sons owe fathers, see also Warren Carter, "God as 'Father' in Matthew: Imperial Intersections," in *Finding a Woman's Place: Essays in Honor of Carolyn Osiek*, ed. David L. Balch and Jason T. Lamoreaux, Princeton Theological Monograph Series (Eugene, OR: Pickwick, 2011), 81–102.

42 Kahl, *Galatians Re-imagined*, 185. The Gospel of Matthew also teaches that sons owe fathers. See Carter, "God as 'Father,'" 96, where he argues that both Rome and Matthew "create a people focused on the Fathers, thereby shaping a community."

43 Kahl, *Galatians Re-imagined*, 185.

44 See Kahl, 220.

45 Elsa Tamez, *Struggles for Power in Early Christianity: A Study of the First Letter to Timothy*, trans. Gloria Kinsler (Maryknoll, NY: Orbis, 2007), 74.

46 See Tamez, 70–74.

47 See Tamez, 72; and Kahl, *Galatians Re-imagined*, 261.

48 For further reflection on early followers of Jesus taking on some of the patriarchal values of Rome, see, e.g., David L. Balch, "Values of Roman Women Including Priests," in Balch and Lamoreaux, *Finding a Woman's Place*, 4, 44.

49 See Tamez, *Struggles for Power*, 27. See also Erik Heen, "Radical Patronage in Luke–Acts," *Currents in Theology and Mission* 33, no. 6 (December 2006): 445–58.

50 See Tamez, *Struggles for Power*, 27–28.

51 See Tamez, 28.

52 Tamez, 27.

53 See Tamez, 28. See chapter 4 on Luther's view of class distinctions and authority for women.

54 Kahl gives insightful commentary on some examples of ancient violent divine fatherhood, including in the Pergamon Altar.

55 Kahl, *Galatians Re-imagined*, 261.

56 Laqueur, *Making Sex*, 96.

57 See Laqueur, 135.

58 See Laqueur, 135–37.

59 Scott Harrison, "California Retrospective: In 1938, L.A. Woman Went to Jail for Wearing Slacks in Courtroom," *Los Angeles Times*, October 23, 2014, accessed December 12, 2021, https://www.latimes.com/local/california/la-me-california-retrospective-20141023-story.html.

80 Alexandra Mondalek, "The History of Women Wearing Pants as Power Symbol," *Huffington Post*, March 2, 2018, updated March 4, 2021, accessed December 12, 2021, https://www.huffpost.com/entry/the-history-of-women-wearing-pants-as-power-symbol_n_5a99bb95e4b0a0ba4ad34fe7.

81 Gwyn Topham, "Female British Airways Cabin Crew Win the Right to Wear Trousers," *Guardian*, February 5, 2016, accessed December 12, 2021, https://www.theguardian.com/business/2016/feb/05/female-british-airways-cabin-crew-win-the-right-to-wear-trousers.

82 Beard, *Women & Power*, 86–87.

83 Evangelical Lutheran Church in America, *Faith, Sexism, and Justice*, 54.

Chapter 3: Fathers—Ruling Sex and Ruling Race

1 See Tina Cassidy, *Mr. President, How Long Must We Wait?* (New York: 37 INK of Simon & Schuster, 2019), 199.

2 Ida B. Wells, as quoted in Cassidy, 55. See Cassidy, 53–55. For contemporary reflections on racism and sexism and the right to vote, see Jeanne Stevenson-Moessner, ed., *Women with 2020 Vision: American Theologians on the Voice, Vote, and Vision of Women* (Minneapolis: Fortress, 2020).

3 See Brooke Kroeger, *Suffragents: How Women Used Men to Get the Vote* (New York: State University of New York, 2017), 3, 6, 27, 77–78, 80; and Cassidy, *Mr. President*, 55.

4 As quoted in Cassidy, *Mr. President*, 30.

5 Grann, *Killers of the Flower Moon*.

6 Rebecca Sims, Deborah Coe, John Hessian, and Kendra Rosencrans, *50th Anniversary of the Ordination of Women: Survey Report* (Chicago: Evangelical Lutheran Church in America, 2022), https://www.elca.org/justiceforwomen.

7 Sims, Coe, Hessian, and Rosencrans, 9–10.

8 For examples and details of these predominant Christian teachings, see my "Idolatry-Critical Justification," 134–52.

9 Londa Schiebinger, *Nature's Body: Gender in the Making of Modern Science* (Boston: Beacon, 1993), 143.

10 See Schiebinger, 143–45.

11 See Schiebinger, 115–20, term on 116. Schiebinger argues race science and sex science are intertwined, even though historians largely treat them as not.

12 Laqueur, *Making Sex*, 149.

13 See Laqueur, 5–6, 11. See also Anne Fausto-Sterling, *Sexing the Body: Gender Politics and the Construction of Sexuality* (New York: Basic, 2000), 1–25.

14 See Schiebinger, *Nature's Body*, 65–71.

15 See Laqueur, *Making Sex*, 3–4.

16 Author Victor Jozé argued in 1895, "A woman exists only through her ovaries." Quoted in Laqueur, 148.

17 William Cowper, *The Anatomy of Humane Bodies* (London: 1737), as quoted in Laqueur, 171, cited in 285n52.

18 Cowper, as quoted in Laqueur, 171, cited in 285n52.

19 Scientists also interpreted other parts of the female anatomy in relation to male bodies and experiences. For example, wombs were said to wander, and doctors made their own conclusions about female sexual pleasure rather than asking women. See Laqueur, 108–10.

20 Patrick Geddes, as quoted in Laqueur, 6.

21 See Laqueur, 154–55. See Fausto-Sterling, *Sexing the Body*, 119, 121–24.

22 Schiebinger, *Nature's Body*, 139–41.

23 See Scheibinger, 126–29, 248n49.

24 See Schiebinger, 120–21.

25 Carl Linnaeus, as quoted in Schiebinger, 120, cited in 245n19.

26 Richard McCausland, "Particulars Relative to the Nature and Customs of the Indians of North America," *Philosophical Transactions of the Royal Society of London* 76 (1786): 229–35, as quoted in Schiebinger, 123, cited in 246n29.

27 One irony is that in the midst of all the arguments about how people with thick beards were superior to all others, Blumenbach (the anatomist and anthropologist who coined the word *Caucasian*) observed that hairlessness was one of the defining features of humans compared to animals. Schiebinger, 125.

28 Immanuel Kant, *Beobachtungen über das Gefühl des Schönen und Erhabenen*, in *Kants Werke*, ed. Wilhelm Dilthey (Berlin: 1900–1919), 2:229–30, as quoted in Schiebinger, 125, cited in 246n35.

29 Schiebinger, 125.

30 Schiebinger, 90–91.

31 Schiebinger, 161.

32 Schiebinger, 160–72.

33 Karen Baker-Fletcher, *Sisters of Dust, Sisters of Spirit: Womanist Wordings on God and Creation* (Minneapolis: Fortress, 1998), 113.

34 Charles Walter Clarke, as quoted in Fausto-Sterling, *Sexing the Body*, 197.

35 See Fausto-Sterling, 197–98.

36 As quoted in Fausto-Sterling, 198.

37 See Fausto-Sterling, 198.

38 As quoted in Fausto-Sterling, 198–99. Ellipsis in the original quotation.

39 Fausto-Sterling, 199.

40 John Stoltenberg, *Refusing to Be a Man: Essays on Sex and Justice* (New York: Penguin, 1990), 67.

41 See Stoltenberg, 60–68, esp. 68.

42 Stoltenberg, 73.

43 Jenson, "Triune Name of God," 93–94.

44 Jenson, 94.

45 See also the outline document "Women's Cultures: Equality and Difference," Plenary Assembly of the Pontifical Council for Culture, February 4–7, 2015, accessed July 6, 2021, http://www.cultura.va/content/dam/cultura/docs/pdf/ Traccia_en.pdf. This is a nonbinding Vatican document, prepared by Roman Catholic women in advance of the 2015 assembly of the Pontifical Council for Culture: "The physicality of women—which makes the world alive, long-living, able to extend itself—finds in the womb its greatest expression."

46 For a helpful critique, see Lois Malcolm, "On Not Three Male Gods: Retrieving Wisdom in Trinitarian Discourse," *Dialog* 49, no. 3 (Fall 2010): 238–47, esp. 243–45.

47 Stoltenberg, *Refusing to Be a Man*, 68.

48 Saint Anselm of Canterbury in Prayer 10 to Saint Paul, "Opera Omnia" in 3:33 and 39–41, based on Matthew 23:37.

49 Much of this section is dependent upon and drawn from Debbie Blue's incisive and comforting book, *Consider the Birds: A Provocative Guide to the Birds of the Bible* (Nashville, TN: Abingdon, 2013), 151–88.

50 Blue, 154.

51 Blue, 155.

Chapter 4: Fathers and Sons, Sex and Empire

1 LW 51:149.

2 LW 26:186–87; WA 401:309–10. Luther lectured on Galatians in 1516–17 and again in 1531; the latter lectures were published in 1535. By 1531, four of Martin and Katharina's six children were born. Although not always the case, the English translation of Luther's Latin in this passage is a faithful rendition. I am grateful to my son Evan Streufert-Wold for his assistance with the Latin texts.

3 Luther also gives an inclusive image of Jesus Christ when he explains parental discipline of Christ, who chastises the Pharisees harshly with the fatherly and motherly "rebukes of a faithful friend." LW 26:188.

4 See LW 51:146–50, esp. 149.

5 LW 26:356 (emphasis added). Of note is that earlier in the passage cited here, Luther illustrates the manner of equality in Christ with other "divinely ordained" offices that are disrupted in Christ, all but one of which is male identified: "neither lady nor servant." See LW 26:353–54.

6 Johannes Schilling, ed., "Brief an den Vater: Martin Luthers Widmungsbrief zu 'De votis monasticis iudicium' (1521)," *Luther* 80, no. 1 (2009): 7.

7   Ian D. Siggins, *Luther and His Mother* (Philadelphia: Fortress, 1981), 74–75.

8   See Schilling, "Brief an den Vater," 8, 10.

9   *LW* 26:97.

10 *LW* 4:24. See also *LW* 4:36 on Sarah's greater understanding of the Promise than Abraham.

11 *LW* 26:97.

12 *TAL* 2:323.

13 See Gordon Jensen, "Introduction," *TAL* 2:259–62.

14 See *TAL* 2:259.

15 *TAL* 2:263–64.

16 *WA* 46:623. Readers of German will note that Luther's German is different from contemporary German.

17 Unless otherwise noted, all translations are mine. In this instance, I have translated the passage to show the meaning in German more clearly.

18 Luther, as quoted in Schilling, "Brief an den Vater," 11.

19 Luther, as quoted in Schilling, 10.

20 *WA* 46:623.

21 See Peter Terrell, *Collins German-English Dictionary* (London: Collins, 1980), 564.

22 Luther, as quoted in Schilling, "Brief an den Vater," 10 (emphasis in original).

23 *WA* 31II:4; *LW* 16:215.

24 See, e.g., *LW* 26:127, 187, 228, 234, 355–56, 380, 385.

25 *LW* 26:345; *WA* 40I:529.

26 *LW* 26:346; *WA* 40I:530.

27 The editors note that other references in Luther's writings indicate "that it was customary for a child to have to kiss the whip after he had been punished." See *LW* 26:345n113.

28 *LW* 26:389–90; *WA* 40I:593–94.

29 See Siggins, *Luther and His Mother*, 5.

30 In Genesis 1:27, the literal translation of the Hebrew is male centric: "For God created man in his image, in the image of God he created him." Modern translations such as the NRSV temper the literal sense by focusing on a more inclusive translation: "So God created *humankind* in his image, in the image of God he created *them*" (emphasis added). Note that the pronouns for God are still male. In contrast, some biblical scholars argue that Genesis 2:7 refers to God's simultaneous formation of two earth creatures. See Phyllis Trible, *God and the Rhetoric of Sexuality* (Philadelphia: Fortress, 1978), 72–81.

31 Heide Wunder, *He Is the Sun, She Is the Moon: Women in Early Modern Germany*, trans. Thomas Dunlap (Cambridge, MA: Harvard University Press, 1998), 148. See also Merry E. Wiesner, *Gender, Church, and State in Early Modern Germany: Essays* (London: Longman, 1998), 91.

32 Wunder, *He Is the Sun*, 151.

33 Wunder, 151; Jane P. Davidson, "Great Black Goats and Evil Little Women: The Image of the Witch in Sixteenth-Century German Art," in *Witchcraft and Demonology in Art and Literature*, ed. Brian P. Levack (New York: Garland, 1992), 45.

34 See Carter Lindberg, "Martin Luther on Marriage and Family," *Perichoresis* 2, no. 1 (2004): 27–46, as cited in *TAL* 2:68.

35 See, e.g., Heinrich Bornkamm, *Luther in Mid-career, 1521–1530*, ed. Karin Bornkamm, trans. E. Theodore Bachmann (Philadelphia: Fortress, 1983), 140–42.

36 For more about his will, see "Luther's Will, 1542," *TAL* 5:9–16.

37 See Kirsi I. Stjerna and Else Marie Wiberg Pedersen, introduction to "Lectures on Genesis 1:26–2:3 and Genesis 2:21–215," *TAL* 6:67–77, esp. 69.

38 See Stjerna and Pedersen, *TAL* 6:73–74.

39 See Stjerna and Pedersen, *TAL* 6:75.

40 See Kristen E. Kvam, "God's Heart Revealed in Eden: Luther on the Character of God and the Vocation of Humanity," in Streufert, *Transformative Lutheran Theologies*, 57–67, 242–43.

41 *LW* 1:178.

42 *LW* 1:179.

43 *LW* 1:193.

44 See Kvam, "God's Heart Revealed," 65–66.

45 *LW* 1:325.

46 The rest of the chapter is based on research previously published in my "Language, Sex, and Luther: Feminist Observations," *Religions* 11, no. 83 (2020): 1–10, https://doi.org/10.3390/rel11020083.

47 *LW* 21:309.

48 See the excerpt from *The Book of Margery Kempe*, as quoted in Emily McLemore, "Thinking Sex, Teaching Violence, and *The Book of Margery Kempe*," *Medieval Studies Research Blog: Meet Us at the Crossroads of Everything*, University of Notre Dame, March 3, 2021, https://sites.nd.edu/manuscript-studies/2021/03/03/thinking-sex-teaching-violence-and-the-book-of-margery-kempe/.

49 Martin Luther, *Martin Luther: Die Hauptschriften, 3 Auflage* (Berlin: Christlicher Zeitschriftenverlag, n.d.), 381.

50 Luther, 373.

51 See *LW* 21:299.

52 Luther, *Die Hauptschriften*, 374.

53 See *LW* 21:312.

54 See *LW* 21:308.

55 *WA* 46:623.

56 *WA* 46:623. See also *WA* 46:619, 621, 622.

57 WA 46:620.
58 WA 46:616.
59 WA 46:616.
60 WA 46:617.
61 Luther, *Die Hauptschriften*, 387.
62 *LW* 21:317.
63 *LW* 21:322.
64 Luther, *Die Hauptschriften*, 391.
65 *LW* 21:313.
66 Luther, *Die Hauptschriften*, 384.
67 *LW* 21:315; Luther, 386.
68 *LW* 21:324; Luther, *Die Hauptschriften*, 392.
69 In German, "man" is distinct from "Mann," with the latter meaning "man" in English.
70 *LW* 21:312.
71 Luther, *Die Hauptschriften*, 384.
72 *LW* 21:312.
73 Luther, *Die Hauptschriften*, 383.
74 Literally, people willing to be paid to rule and work on someone else's orders.
75 See Laqueur, *Making Sex*, 58.

Chapter 5: Patriarchy and (the) Tradition

1 See, e.g., TAL 2:34.
2 TAL 2:300.
3 *LW* 26:89.
4 Martin Luther, "An Introduction to St. Paul's Letter to the Romans," in Luther's German Bible of 1522, *Dr. Martin Luther's vermischte deutsche Schriften*, vol. 63, ed. Johann K. Irmischer, trans. Robert E. Smith (Erlangen, Germany: Heyder & Zimmer, 1854), 124–25, https://christian.net/pub/resources/text/wittenberg/luther/luther-faith.txt.
5 Luther, 124–25.
6 *LW* 26:38.
7 TAL 2:302–03.
8 Mary Daly is famous for saying, "If God is male, then male is God." See Daly, *Beyond God the Father*, 19. For a more academic explanation of language for God through Luther's ideas, see my "A Word of the Word for Our Hearts: Embracing Multiply-Gendered God Language with Luther," in *The Alternative Luther: Lutheran Theology from the Subaltern*, ed. Else Marie Wiberg Pedersen (Lanham, MD: Lexington / Fortress Academic, 2019), 106; and my article "Language."

9   Evangelical Lutheran Church in America, *Faith, Sexism, and Justice*, 3–4.

10 See the interview with Krista Tippett, "Unfolding Language, Unfolding Life," *On Being with Krista Tippett*, original air date November 3, 2011, updated February 4, 2016, http://onbeing.org/programs/jean-berko-gleason-unfolding -language-unfolding-life/.

11 Kate Swift and Casey Miller, *The Handbook of Nonsexist Writing: For Writers, Editors and Speakers*, 2nd ed. (Lincoln, NE: iUniverse, 2000), 8.

12 Jean Berko Gleason, "The Acquisition of Routines in Child Language," *Language in Society* 5 (1976): 129–36.

13 See Swift and Miller, *Handbook*, 4.

14 LW 26:220.

15 Gracia Grindal, "Reflections on God 'the Father,'" *Word & World* 4, no. 1 (1984): 79.

16 Much of the following sections on the language of faith and the Word of God come from my chapter "Word of the Word," 103–17.

17 See David Steinmetz, "Luther, the Reformers, and the Bible," in *Living Traditions of the Bible: Scripture in Jewish, Christian, and Muslim Practice*, ed. James E. Bowley (St. Louis: Chalice, 1999), 173–74.

18 See Robert Goeser, "Luther: Word of God, Language, and Art," *Currents in Theology and Mission* 18, no. 1 (February 1991): 9.

19 See TAL 2:165.

20 TAL 2:148.

21 TAL 2:148–49. See also Kathryn A. Kleinhans, "The Word Made Words: A Lutheran Perspective on the Authority and Use of the Scriptures," *Word & World* 26, no. 4 (Fall 2006): 402–11.

22 TAL 2:147.

23 TAL 2:147.

24 LW 38:198.

25 See LW 40:79–101.

26 See Goeser, "Luther," 6–11, esp. 6. See LW 51:85.

27 LW 38:242.

28 Martin Luther, *Luther's Correspondence and Other Contemporary Letters*, trans. and ed. Preserved Smith and Charles M. Jacobs (Philadelphia: Lutheran Publication Society, 1918), 2:176, 177.

29 LW 32:196. See also 195–201; Volker Leppin, introduction to TAL 6:19–22.

30 LW 35:218.

31 See Streufert, "Word of the Word," 109.

32 Steinmetz, "Luther, the Reformers," 168.

33 Lydia Saad, "Record Few Americans Believe Bible Is Literal Word of God," Gallup, May 15, 2017, https://news.gallup.com/poll/210704/record-few-americans -believe-bible-literal-word-god.aspx.

34 Jerry Jacobs Jr., "Christ: The Original Catholic Alpha," Catholic Alpha, accessed December 15, 2021, https://catholicalpha.com/christ-the-original-catholic-alpha.

35 See, e.g., TAL 2:95; 2:268n30; and 2:393.

36 TAL 2:312.

37 In a similar vein, Vítor Westhelle referred to the church as event. See his The Church Event: Call and Challenge of a Church Protestant (Minneapolis: Fortress, 2009).

38 Womanist theologian Delores S. Williams explores this image of God in Sisters in the Wilderness.

39 Deut 32:11–12.

40 Feminist theologian Rosemary Radford Ruether explores this idea in To Change the World: Christology and Cultural Criticism (New York: Crossroad, 1983).

41 LW 35:121.

42 Luther, as quoted in Kleinhans, "Word Made Words," 407.

43 See, e.g., LW 38:39–40, 44.

44 LW 26:77; WA 40:147–49.

45 LW 26:392; WA 40:597.

46 See, e.g., LW 26:45, 58; WA 40:102, 103, 120, 121.

47 LW 17:139. See also LW 26:47; WA 40:104–6.

48 LW 35:344.

49 See LW 26:38; WA 40:91, 92.

50 See LW 38:198.

51 See LW 26:25; WA 40:70, 71.

52 See LW 26:24–25; WA 40:68–70, 71.

53 LW 26:64; WA 40:129, 130.

54 TAL 3:118, 116.

55 TAL 3:119.

56 LW 38:198.

57 See LW 38:99.

58 LW 38:56.

59 LW 49:359. See also how Luther talked about Abraham and Sarah's faith as joyful in LW 3:154.

60 See Christine Helmer, "The Experience of Justification," in Justification in a Post-Christian Society, Church of Sweden Research Series, vol. 8, ed. Carl-Henric Grenholm and Göran Gunner (Eugene, OR: Pickwick, 2014), 36–56, esp. 52.

61 See, e.g., Lois Malcolm, "The Gospel and Feminist Theology: A Proposal for Lutheran Dogmatics," Word & World 15, no. 3 (Summer 1995): 290–98; and Ted Peters, God—the World's Future, 3rd ed. (Minneapolis: Fortress, 2015), 421–34, esp. 422–23, 430.

82 See my "Idolatry-Critical Justification," 144–46.
83 *LW* 38:107.

Chapter 6: Transformative Theology

1 See, e.g., Kenneth G. Appold, introduction to Luther's "Preface to the New Testament," *TAL* 6:414–15.
2 See, e.g., Brooks Schramm, introduction to "Preface to the Old Testament. 1545 (1523)," *TAL* 6:41–46.
3 *TAL* 6:30. For "jackasses," see 6:29–30.
4 *TAL* 2:30.
5 See Kahl, *Galatians Re-imagined*, 69–71.
6 Similar but less overtly gendered images within the United States are statues and paintings of defeated American Indians.
7 For a fuller explanation and photos of these and other visual representations in Imperial Rome, see Davina C. Lopez, *Apostle to the Conquered: Reimagining Paul's Mission*, Paul in Critical Contexts (Minneapolis: Fortress, 2010). For the carvings at Aphrodisias, see 42–45.
8 See, e.g., Kahl, *Galatians Re-imagined*, 125–26, 170.
9 Kahl, 150–51.
10 See Kahl's description of normalized violence in the Pergamon Altar and elsewhere in Rome.
11 See my "For the Woman Who Yelled 'Fire!' in My Backyard: Rape Law and Lutheran Theology," in *Lutheran Theology and Secular Law: The Work of the Modern State*, ed. Marie A. Failinger and Ronald W. Duty (New York: Rowman & Littlefield, 2018), 138–49.
12 See my "Idolatry-Critical Justification," 134–52; and "Solus Christus within Empire: Christology in the Face of Violence against Women," *Dialog: A Journal of Theology* 53, no. 3 (Fall 2014): 223–32.
13 Kahl, *Galatians Re-imagined*, 222.
14 Brigitte Kahl, "Galatians: On Discomfort about Gender and Other Problems of Otherness," in *Feminist Biblical Interpretation: A Compendium of Critical Commentary on the Books of the Bible and Related Literature*, ed. Luise Schottroff and Marie-Theres Wacker, trans. Lisa E. Dahill et al. (Grand Rapids, MI: Eerdmans, 2012), 762–64.
15 See Lopez, *Apostle to the Conquered*, 141–46.
16 Lopez, 142.
17 Lopez 145.
18 See Lopez, 143–46.

19 Lopez, 141.

20 See Lopez, 55.

21 Carolyn Pressler, "Deuteronomy," in *Women's Bible Commentary*, 3rd ed., 20th anniversary ed., ed. Carol A. Newsom, Sharon H. Ringe, and Jacqueline E. Lapsley (Louisville: Westminster John Knox, 2012), 88–102.

22 See S. Dean McBride Jr., "Deuteronomy: Introduction," in *HarperCollins Study Bible*, ed. Wayne A. Meeks (New York: HarperCollins, 1993), 266–68.

23 TAL 6:51.

24 McBride, "Deuteronomy," 318.

25 Deut 32:11–12, as quoted in Natan Slifkin, "On Eagles' Wings," Rationalist Judaism, February 4, 2016, http://www.rationalistjudaism.com/search?q=Deut +32%3A11-12.

26 See "Griffon Vultures Documentary," Planet Doc, May 24, 2016, https://www .bing.com/videos/search?q=griffon+vultures&docid=607999436040201168 &mid=B586318D326436CE4F97B586318D326436CE4F97&view=detail& FORM=VIRE.

27 "Shock as Rare 'Male' Vulture Lays an Egg at Wildlife Sanctuary," BBC, January 26, 2018, https://www.bbc.com/news/uk-england-kent-42835688.

28 Michaela Bose and Francois Sarrazin, "Competitive Behaviour and Feeding Rate in a Reintroduced Population of Griffon Vultures *Gyps fulvus*," *British Ornithologists' Union* 149, no. 3 (2007): 490–501, https://doi.org/10.1111/j.1474 -919X.2007.00674.x.

29 See Melissa Mayntz, "20 Fun Facts about Vultures: Trivia about Vultures, Buzzards, and Condors," Spruce, updated March 19, 2021, https://www.thespruce .com/fun-facts-about-vultures-385520.

30 See "Griffon Vulture," Animalia, https://animalia.bio/griffon-vulture#.

31 See "New Vulture Chick at the Zoo," City of Albuquerque, February 28, 2018, https://www.cabq.gov/artsculture/biopark/news/new-vulture-chick-at-the -zoo; see also "Griffon Vulture."

32 Pressler, "Deuteronomy," 102. Paul claims the same sense of being in the travail of labor in Galatians 4:19.

33 See, e.g., Kathleen M. O'Connor, "Jeremiah," in *Women's Bible Commentary*, 267–70.

34 See Corrine Carvalho, "Whose Gendered Language of God? Contemporary Gender Theory and Divine Gender in the Prophets," *Currents in Theology and Mission* 43, no. 3 (July 2016): 12–16. https://www.currentsjournal.org/index .php/currents/article/view/33.

35 Carvalho, 13.

36 Carvalho, 13, with reference to I. Zsolnay, "The Misconstrued Role of the *Assinu* in Ancient Near Eastern Prophecy," in *Prophets Male and Female: Gender*

and Prophecy in the Hebrew Bible, the Eastern Mediterranean, and the Ancient Near East, ed. Jonathan Stökl and Corrine L. Carvalho (Atlanta: Society of Biblical Literature, 2013), 81–99.

37 Carvalho, "Whose Gendered Language of God?," 13.

38 Carvalho, 14.

39 Carvalho, 15.

40 See Carvalho, 15.

41 See Sandra M. Schneiders, "The Footwashing (John 13:1–20): An Experiment in Hermeneutics," *Catholic Biblical Quarterly* 43 (January 1981): 76–92; and Luise Schottroff, Silvia Schroer, and Marie-Theres Wacker, *Feminist Interpretation: The Bible in Women's Perspective*, trans. Martin and Barbara Rumscheidt (Minneapolis: Fortress, 1998), 232.

42 Ruth Habermann, "Gospel of John," in *Feminist Biblical Interpretation*, 672–74.

43 See Carol Schersten LaHurd, "Re-viewing Luke 15 with Arab Christian Women," in *A Feminist Companion to Luke*, ed. Amy-Jill Levine with Marianne Blickenstaff (Cleveland, OH: Pilgrim, 2004), 256.

44 Mary Rose D'Angelo, "The ANHP Question in Luke–Acts: Imperial Masculinity and the Deployment of Women in the Early Second Century," in Levine with Blickenstaff, *Feminist Companion*, 45.

45 See, e.g., Jane D. Schaberg and Sharon H. Ringe, "Gospel of Luke," in *Women's Bible Commentary*, 498; D'Angelo, 68.

46 Schaberg and Ringe, "Gospel of Luke," 493.

47 Luise Schottroff, *The Parables of Jesus*, trans. Linda M. Maloney (Minneapolis: Fortress, 2006), 153.

48 Schottroff, 154.

49 Kahl, in Levine with Blickenstaff, *Feminist Companion*, 74.

50 Kahl, in Levine with Blickenstaff, 72.

51 Kahl, in Levine with Blickenstaff, 79.

52 Kahl, in Levine with Blickenstaff, 80.

53 LaHurd, "Re-viewing Luke 15," 257.

54 See LaHurd, 257.

55 Schottroff, *Parables of Jesus*, 154.

Bibliography

American Lutheran Church, Church Council Action 76.6.119. Church Council and Executive Council Minutes (TALC 8/2). Elk Grove Village, IL: Archives of the Evangelical Lutheran Church in America, June 14–18, 1976.

Anselm of Canterbury, Saint. *The Prayers and Meditations of Saint Anselm with the Proslogion*. Translated by Sister Benedicta Ward, SLG. London: Penguin, 1973.

Arefin, D. Sharmin. "Is Hair Discrimination Race Discrimination?" American Bar Association, April 17, 2020. https://www.americanbar.org/groups/business_law/publications/blt/2020/05/hair-discrimination.

Baker-Fletcher, Karen. *Sisters of Dust, Sisters of Spirit: Womanist Wordings on God and Creation*. Minneapolis: Fortress, 1998.

Balch, David L., and Jason T. Lamoreaux, eds. *Finding a Woman's Place: Essays in Honor of Carolyn Osiek*. Princeton Theological Monograph Series. Eugene, OR: Pickwick, 2011.

Beard, Mary. *Women & Power: A Manifesto*. New York: Liveright, 2017.

Berko Gleason, Jean. "The Acquisition of Routines in Child Language." *Language in Society* 5 (1976): 129–136.

Bloesch, Donald G. *The Battle for the Trinity: The Debate over Inclusive God-Language*. Ann Arbor, MI: Vine, 1985.

Blue, Debbie. *Consider the Birds: A Provocative Guide to the Birds of the Bible*. Nashville, TN: Abingdon, 2013.

Bornkamm, Heinrich. *Luther in Mid-career, 1521–1530*. Edited by Karin Bornkamm. Translated by E. Theodore Bachmann. Philadelphia: Fortress, 1983.

Bose, Michaela, and Francois Sarrazin. "Competitive Behaviour and Feeding Rate in a Reintroduced Population of Griffon Vultures *Gyps fulvus*." *British Ornithologists' Union* 149, no. 3 (2007): 490–501. https://doi.org/10.1111/j.1474-919X.2007.00674.x.

Braaten, Carl E., and Robert W. Jenson, eds. *Christian Dogmatics.* Vol. 1. Philadelphia: Fortress, 1984.

British Broadcasting Corporation (BBC). "Shock as Rare 'Male' Vulture Lays an Egg at Wildlife Sanctuary." January 26, 2018. https://www.bbc.com/news/uk-england -kent-42835688.

Bynum, Caroline Walker. *Fragmentation and Redemption: Essays on Gender and the Human Body in Medieval Religion.* New York: Zone, 1992.

Carter, Jimmy. *A Call to Action: Women, Religion, Violence, and Power.* New York: Simon & Schuster, 2014.

Carvalho, Corrine. "Whose Gendered Language of God? Contemporary Gender The-ory and Divine Gender in the Prophets." *Currents in Theology and Mission* 43, no. 3 (July 2016): 12–16. https://www.currentsjournal.org/index.php/currents/article/ view/33.

Cassidy, Tina. *Mr. President, How Long Must We Wait?* New York: 37 INK of Simon & Schuster, 2019.

Centers for Disease Control. "Racial and Ethnic Disparities Continue in Pregnancy-Related Deaths." Press release, September 5, 2019. https://www.cdc.gov/media/ releases/2019/p0905-racial-ethnic-disparities-pregnancy-deaths.html.

Christ, Carol. *Rebirth of the Goddess: Finding Meaning in Feminist Spirituality.* New York: Routledge, 1997.

City of Albuquerque. "New Vulture Chick at the Zoo." February 28, 2018. https://www .cabq.gov/artsculture/biopark/news/new-vulture-chick-at-the-zoo.

Cone, James H. *The Cross and the Lynching Tree.* Maryknoll, NY: Orbis, 2011.

———. *God of the Oppressed.* New York: Seabury, 1975.

Crenshaw, Kimberlé. "Demarginalizing the Intersection of Race and Sex: A Black Fem-inist Critique of Antidiscrimination Doctrine, Feminist Theory and Antiracist Politics." *University of Chicago Legal Forum* (1989): 139–67.

Crossan, John Dominic. *The Essential Jesus: Original Sayings and Earliest Images.* New York: HarperSanFrancisco, 1994.

———. *Jesus: A Revolutionary Biography.* New York: HarperSanFrancisco, 1994.

Daly, Mary. *Beyond God the Father: Toward a Philosophy of Women's Liberation.* Boston: Beacon, 1973.

———. *Gyn/Ecology: The Metaethics of Radical Freedom.* Boston: Beacon, 1978.

Davidson, Jane P. "Great Black Goats and Evil Little Women: The Image of the Witch in Sixteenth-Century German Art." In *Witchcraft and Demonology in Art and Liter-ature,* edited by Brian P. Levack, 45–61. New York: Garland, 1992.

Davis, Angela Y. *Women, Race, and Class.* New York: Vintage, 1983.

Euripides. *Trojan Women.* Edited and translated by Paul D. Streufert. Peterborough, Canada: Broadview, 2021.

Evangelical Lutheran Church in America. *Faith, Sexism, and Justice: A Call to Action.* Chicago: Evangelical Lutheran Church in America, 2019. https://download.elca .org/ELCA%20Resource%20Repository/Faith_Sexism_Justice_Social _Statement_Adopted.pdf?_ga=2.68621905.1110212823.1631894531-1092238982 .1556124288.

Fausto-Sterling, Anne. *Sexing the Body: Gender Politics and the Construction of Sexuality.* New York: Basic, 2000.

Gates, Melinda. *The Moment of Lift: How Empowering Women Changes the World.* New York: Flatiron, 2019.

Goeser, Robert. "Luther: Word of God, Language, and Art." *Currents in Theology and Mission* 18, no. 1 (February 1991): 6–11.

Grann, David. *Killers of the Flower Moon: The Osage Murders and the Birth of the FBI.* New York: Vintage, 2017.

Grant, Jacquelyn. *White Women's Christ and Black Women's Jesus: Feminist Christology and Womanist Response.* American Academy of Religion Academy Series 64, edited by Susan Thistlethwaite. Atlanta: Scholars, 1989.

Grindal, Gracia. "Reflections on God 'the Father.'" *Word & World* 4, no. 1 (1984): 78–86.

Harrison, Scott. "California Retrospective: In 1938, L.A. Woman Went to Jail for Wearing Slacks in Courtroom." *Los Angeles Times,* October 23, 2014. https://www.latimes .com/local/california/la-me-california-retrospective-20141023-story.html.

Heen, Erik. "Radical Patronage in Luke–Acts." *Currents in Theology and Mission* 33, no. 6 (December 2006): 445–458.

Helmer, Christine. "The Experience of Justification." In *Justification in a Post-Christian Society,* Church of Sweden Research Series, vol. 8, edited by Carl-Henric Grenholm and Göran Gunner, 36–56. Eugene, OR: Pickwick, 2014.

Hinlicky, Paul R. *Beloved Community: Critical Dogmatics after Christendom.* Grand Rapids, MI: Eerdmans, 2015.

Hong Kingston, Maxine. *The Woman Warrior.* 1975. Reprint, London: Picador, 2015.

John Paul II (Pope). *Mulieris Dignitatem.* Rome: Libreria Editrice Vaticana, 1988. https:// www.vatican.va/content/john-paul-ii/en/apost_letters/1988/documents/hf_jp -ii_apl_19880815_mulieris-dignitatem.html.

Johnson, Elizabeth A. *She Who Is: The Mystery of God in Feminist Theological Discourse.* New York: Crossroad, 1994.

Kahl, Brigitte. *Galatians Re-imagined: Reading with the Eyes of the Vanquished.* Paul in Critical Contexts. Minneapolis: Fortress, 2010.

Kleinhans, Kathryn A. "The Word Made Words: A Lutheran Perspective on the Authority and Use of the Scriptures." *Word & World* 26, no. 4 (Fall 2006): 402–411.

Kroeger, Brooke. *Suffragents: How Women Used Men to Get the Vote.* New York: State University of New York, 2017.

Laqueur, Thomas. *Making Sex: Body and Gender from the Greeks to Freud.* Cambridge, MA: Harvard University Press, 1990.

Levine, Amy-Jill, with Marianne Blickenstaff, eds. *A Feminist Companion to Luke.* Cleveland: Pilgrim, 2001.

Lewis, Charlton T. *Elementary Latin Dictionary.* New York: American Book, 1918.

Lopez, Davina C. *Apostle to the Conquered: Reimagining Paul's Mission.* Paul in Critical Contexts. Minneapolis: Fortress, 2010.

Luther, Martin. *The Annotated Luther.* Edited by Hans J. Hillerbrand, Kirsi I. Stjerna, and Timothy J. Wengert. 6 vols. Minneapolis: Fortress, 2015–2017.

———. *D. Martin Luthers Werke: Kritische Gesamtausgabe.* Edited by J. K. F. Knaake. 109 vols. Weimar: H. Böhlau, 1883–2009.

———. *Dr. Martin Luther's vermischte deutsche Schriften.* Vol. 63, edited by Johann K. Irmischer, translated by Robert E. Smith. Erlangen, Germany: Heyder & Zimmer, 1854. https://christian.net/pub/resources/text/wittenberg/luther/luther-faith.txt.

———. *Luther's Correspondence and Other Contemporary Letters.* Vol. 2, translated and edited by Preserved Smith and Charles M. Jacobs. Philadelphia: Lutheran Publication Society, 1918.

———. *Luther's Works.* American Edition. Edited by Helmut T. Lehmann and Jaroslav Pelikan. 55 vols. St. Louis: Concordia; Philadelphia: Fortress, 1955–1986.

———. *Martin Luther: Die Hauptschriften, 3 Auflage.* Berlin: Christlicher Zeitschriftenverlag, n.d.

Malcolm, Lois. "The Gospel and Feminist Theology: A Proposal for Lutheran Dogmatics." *Word & World* 15, no. 3 (Summer 1995): 290–298.

———. "On Not Three Male Gods: Retrieving Wisdom in Trinitarian Discourse." *Dialog* 49, no. 3 (Fall 2010): 238–247.

Maseno, Loreen, and Elia Shabani Mligo. *Women within Religions: Patriarchy, Feminism, and the Role of Women in Selected World Religions.* Eugene, OR: Wipf & Stock, 2019.

Mayntz, Melissa. "20 Fun Facts about Vultures: Trivia about Vultures, Buzzards, and Condors." Spruce. Updated March 19, 2021. https://www.thespruce.com/fun-facts-about -vultures-385520.

McBride, S. Dean, Jr. "Deuteronomy: Introduction." In *HarperCollins Study Bible*, edited by Wayne A. Meeks, 266–268. New York: HarperCollins, 1993.

McGuire, Danielle L. *At the Dark End of the Street.* New York: Knopf, 2010.

McLemore, Emily. "Thinking Sex, Teaching Violence, and *The Book of Margery Kempe.*" *Medieval Studies Research Blog: Meet Us at the Crossroads of Everything*, University of Notre Dame, March 3, 2021. https://sites.nd.edu/manuscript-studies/2021/03/03/ thinking-sex-teaching-violence-and-the-book-of-margery-kempe/.

Mondalek, Alexandra. "The History of Women Wearing Pants as Power Symbol." *Huffington Post*, March 2, 2018. https://www.huffpost.com/entry/the-history-of-women -wearing-pants-as-power-symbol_n_5a99bb95e4b0a0ba4ad34fe7.

National Conference of State Legislatures. "Breastfeeding State Laws." August 26, 2021. https://www.ncsl.org/research/health/breastfeeding-state-laws.aspx.

Neuenfeldt, Elaine, ed. *Gender Justice Policy*. Geneva: Lutheran World Federation, 2013. https://www.lutheranworld.org/sites/default/files/DTPW-WICAS_Gender _Justice.pdf.

Newsom, Carol A., Sharon H. Ringe, and Jacqueline E. Lapsley, eds. *Women's Bible Commentary*. 3rd ed. 20th anniversary ed. Louisville: Westminster John Knox, 2012.

Office of the Secretary and the Commission for Communication. *Guidelines for Inclusive Use of the English Language for Speakers, Writers and Editors*. Chicago: Evangelical Lutheran Church in America, 1989.

Park, Katharine, with Robert A. Nye. "Destiny Is Anatomy." *New Republic*, February 18, 1991.

Peters, Ted. *God—the World's Future*. 3rd ed. Minneapolis: Fortress, 2015.

Planet Doc. "Griffon Vultures Documentary." May 24, 2016. https://www.bing.com/ videos/search?q=griffon+vultures&docid=607999436040201168&mid=B586318D32 6436CE4F97B586318D326436CE4F97&view=detail&FORM=VIRE.

Plenary Assembly of the Pontifical Council for Culture. "Women's Cultures: Equality and Difference." February 4–7, 2015. http://www.cultura.va/content/dam/cultura/ docs/pdf/Traccia_en.pdf.

Radford Ruether, Rosemary. *To Change the World: Christology and Cultural Criticism*. New York: Crossroad, 1983.

Ramshaw Schmidt, Gail. "*De Divinis nominibus*: The Gender of God." *Worship* 56 (March 1982): 117–131.

Reisz, H. Frederick, Jr. "Language and God: Theological and Pastoral Issues." In *Women and Men in the Body of Christ: A Report by the Advisory Committee for the Study on Women and Men in the Body of Christ*, 83–93. New York: Lutheran Church in America, 1987.

Schiebinger, Londa. *Nature's Body: Gender in the Making of Modern Science*. Boston: Beacon, 1993.

Schilling, Johannes, ed. "Brief an den Vater: Martin Luthers Widmungsbrief zu 'De votis monasticis iudicium' (1521)." *Luther* 80, no. 1 (2009): 2–11.

Schjonberg, Mary Frances, and Melodie Woerman. "Convention Approves Use of Expansive-Language Version of Rite II Eucharistic Prayers." Episcopal News Service, July 12, 2018. https://www.episcopalnewsservice.org/2018/07/12/convention -approves-use-of-expansive-language-version-of-rite-ii-eucharistic-prayers.

Schneiders, Sandra M. "The Footwashing (John 13:1–20): An Experiment in Hermeneutics." *Catholic Biblical Quarterly* 43 (January 1981): 76–92.

Schottroff, Luise. *The Parables of Jesus*. Translated by Linda M. Maloney. Minneapolis: Fortress, 2006.

Schottroff, Luise, Silvia Schroer, and Marie-Theres Wacker. *Feminist Interpretation: The Bible in Women's Perspective*. Translated by Martin and Barbara Rumscheidt. Minneapolis: Fortress, 1998.

Schottroff, Luise, and Marie-Theres Wacker, eds. *Feminist Biblical Interpretation: A Compendium of Critical Commentary on the Books of the Bible and Related Literature*. Translated by Lisa E. Dahill, Everett R. Kalin, Nancy Lukens, Linda M. Maloney, Barbara Rumscheidt, Martin Rumscheidt, and Tina Steiner. Grand Rapids, MI: Eerdmans, 2012.

Schüssler Fiorenza, Elisabeth. *But She Said: Feminist Practices of Biblical Interpretation*. Boston: Beacon, 1992.

Siggins, Ian D. *Luther and His Mother*. Philadelphia: Fortress, 1981.

Sims, Rebecca, Deborah Coe, John Hessian, and Kendra Rosencrans. *50th Anniversary of the Ordination of Women: Survey Report*. Chicago: Evangelical Lutheran Church in America, 2022. https://www.elca.org/justiceforwomen.

Slifkin, Natan. "On Eagles' Wings." Rationalist Judaism, February 4, 2016. http://www.rationalistjudaism.com/search?q=Deut+32%3A11-12.

Steinmetz, David. "Luther, the Reformers, and the Bible." In *Living Traditions of the Bible: Scripture in Jewish, Christian, and Muslim Practice*, edited by James E. Bowley, 163–176. St. Louis: Chalice, 1999.

Stern, Carly. "Six Black Women Detail the Horrific Discrimination They've Faced Because of Their HAIR—Revealing How They Were FIRED from Jobs for Wearing Natural Styles, or Forced to Spend Hundreds of Dollars to Keep Their Locks Straight." *Daily Mail*, August 25, 2020. https://www.dailymail.co.uk/femail/article-8662305/Six-black-women-horrific-discrimination-faced-hair.html.

Stevenson-Moessner, Jeanne, ed. *Women with 2020 Vision: American Theologians on the Voice, Vote, and Vision of Women*. Minneapolis: Fortress, 2020.

Stoltenberg, John. *Refusing to Be a Man: Essays on Sex and Justice*. New York: Penguin, 1990.

Streufert, Mary J. "For the Woman Who Yelled 'Fire!' in My Backyard: Rape Law and Lutheran Theology." In *Lutheran Theology and Secular Law: The Work of the Modern State*, edited by Marie A. Failinger and Ronald W. Duty, 138–149. New York: Rowman & Littlefield, 2018.

———. "Idolatry-Critical Justification and the Foreclosed Gendered Life." In *Lutheran Identity and Political Theology*, edited by Carl-Henric Grenholm and Göran Gunner, 134–152. Church of Sweden Research Series 9. Eugene, OR: Pickwick, 2014.

———. "Language: Idolatry and Evangelism." *Currents in Theology and Mission* 43, no. 3 (July 2016): 3–7. http://www.currentsjournal.org/index.php/currents/issue/view/4.

———. "Language, Sex, and Luther: Feminist Observations." *Religions* 11, no. 83 (2020): 1–10. https://doi.org/10.3390/rel11020083.

———. "Solus Christus within Empire: Christology in the Face of Violence against Women." *Dialog: A Journal of Theology* 53, no. 3 (Fall 2014): 223–232.

———, ed. *Transformative Lutheran Theologies: Feminist, Womanist, and Mujerista Perspectives*. Minneapolis: Fortress, 2010.

———. "A Word of the Word for Our Hearts: Embracing Multiply-Gendered God Language with Luther." In *The Alternative Luther: Lutheran Theology from the Subaltern*, edited by Else Marie Wiberg Pedersen, 103–117. Lanham, MD: Lexington / Fortress Academic, 2019.

Swift, Kate, and Casey Miller. *The Handbook of Nonsexist Writing: For Writers, Editors and Speakers*. 2nd ed. Lincoln, NE: iUniverse, 2000.

Tamez, Elsa. *Struggles for Power in Early Christianity: A Study of the First Letter to Timothy*. Translated by Gloria Kinsler. Maryknoll, NY: Orbis, 2007.

Terrell, Peter. *Collins German-English Dictionary*. London: Collins, 1980.

Tippett, Krista. "Unfolding Language, Unfolding Life." *On Being with Krista Tippett*. Original airdate November 3, 2011. Updated February 4, 2016. http://onbeing.org/programs/jean-berko-gleason-unfolding-language-unfolding-life/.

Topham, Gwyn. "Female British Airways Cabin Crew Win the Right to Wear Trousers." *Guardian*, February 5, 2016. https://www.theguardian.com/business/2016/feb/05/female-british-airways-cabin-crew-win-the-right-to-wear-trousers.

Trible, Phyllis. *God and the Rhetoric of Sexuality*. Philadelphia: Fortress, 1978.

United Church of Christ. "General Synod Inclusive Language." https://www.ucc.org/who-we-are/about/general-synod/worship_inclusive-language_general-synod-inclusive/.

———. "Inclusive Language Resources." https://www.ucc.org/what-we-do/justice-local-church-ministries/local-church/mesa-ministerial-excellence-support-and-authorization/ministers/ministers_local-church-leaders/worship_inclusive-language/worship_inclusive-language_inclusive-language-resources/.

Westhelle, Vítor. *The Church Event: Call and Challenge of a Church Protestant*. Minneapolis: Fortress, 2009.

Wiesner, Merry E. *Gender, Church, and State in Early Modern Germany: Essays*. London: Longman, 1998.

Wilde, Oscar. *The Picture of Dorian Gray*. 1891. Reprint, New York: Dover, 1993.

Wilkerson, Isabel. *Caste: The Origins of Our Discontent*. New York: Random House, 2020.

Williams, Delores. *Sisters in the Wilderness: The Challenges of Womanist God-Talk*. Maryknoll, NY: Orbis, 1993.

Williams-Harris, Deanese. "Racism's Toll on Black Women Includes Staggering Maternal Death Rates." *Chicago Tribune*, May 3, 2021. https://www.chicagotribune.com/living/health/ct-black-maternal-health-week-advocacy-tt-20210503-o4n6ovxlufazpbx4yype6tv6l4-story.html.

Wren, Brian. *What Language Shall I Borrow? God-Talk in Worship: A Male Response to Feminist Theology.* New York: Crossroad, 1989.

Wunder, Heide. *He Is the Sun, She Is the Moon: Women in Early Modern Germany.* Translated by Thomas Dunlap. Cambridge, MA: Harvard University Press, 1998.

Zsolnay, I. "The Misconstrued Role of the *Assinu* in Ancient Near Eastern Prophecy." In *Prophets Male and Female: Gender and Prophecy in the Hebrew Bible, the Eastern Mediterranean, and the Ancient Near East,* edited by Jonathan Stökl and Corrine L. Carvalho, 81–99. Atlanta: Society of Biblical Literature, 2013.

Acknowledgments

First, I would like to thank Fortress Press and the editorial team for supporting this book. My editor, Scott Tunseth, has been immeasurably patient and wise during a tight process. Thank you.

I am also grateful for all the people over many years who have discussed language for God with me and told me their stories. I am grateful for all the scholars on whose work I depend, whether we agree or disagree. Thanks also go to the ELCA task force members who talked and wept and struggled together over language. I am grateful for the sabbatical the churchwide organization of the ELCA granted me to complete the first draft and for my colleagues there who gave me time and patience as I completed this manuscript.

Every author needs such people behind them, but they also need friends and family to support them. I relied on many people, and I am able only to name some of them. Thanks go to Jeannie Kapple, Johanna Johnson, and Tara Meyer Dull for reading early drafts and talking and dreaming with me. Jeannie Kapple and Dane Johnson gave me a beautiful space to work for a month, laced with friendship and care. And I am always and ever grateful for the support and love of my husband, Doug Wold, and our children, Jules, Evan, and Mattias. You keep me laughing.

ACKNOWLEDGMENTS

Subject Index

Selected Scripture Index